KATE TUCKER

MATHEMATICS THROUGH PLAY in the EARLY YEARS

Third Edition

$\circledS$SAGE

Los Angeles | London | New Delhi
Singapore | Washington DC

⑤SAGE

Los Angeles | London | New Delhi
Singapore | Washington DC

SAGE Publications Ltd
1 Oliver's Yard
55 City Road
London EC1Y 1SP

SAGE Publications Inc.
2455 Teller Road
Thousand Oaks, California 91320

SAGE Publications India Pvt Ltd
B 1/I 1 Mohan Cooperative Industrial Area
Mathura Road
New Delhi 110 044

SAGE Publications Asia-Pacific Pte Ltd
3 Church Street
#10-04 Samsung Hub
Singapore 049483

Editor: Jude Bowen
Associate Editor: Miriam Davey
Production editor: Thea Watson
Copyeditor: Sharon Cawood
Proofreader: Nicola Marshall
Indexer: Anne Solamito
Marketing manager: Lorna Patkai
Cover designer: Wendy Scott
Typeset by: C&M Digitals (P) Ltd, Chennai, India
Printed in India by Replika Press Pvt Ltd

Library of Congress Control Number: 2013939739

British Library Cataloguing in Publication data

A catalogue record for this book is available from
the British Library

ISBN 978-1-44626-977-0 pb
ISBN 978-1-44626-976-3 hb

MATHEMATICS THROUGH PLAY in the EARLY YEARS

Contents

About the author

Trained for working with nursery and lower primary-aged children, Kate Tucker specializes in early years teaching with a particular interest in early years mathematics. She is Assistant Head Teacher and early years teacher at Great Torrington Bluecoat Church of England Primary School and Early Years Teaching Centre in Devon, where she also writes and facilitates training on a range of early years themes for practitioners. Kate has taught children aged 3 to 8 for over 20 years and has written widely on early years mathematics and Foundation Stage practice. She has worked within Devon as Leading Maths Teacher, Foundation Stage Leading Maths Teacher and Leading Foundation Stage Teacher. She has also taught the mathematics module for Early Childhood Studies BEd students at the University of Plymouth.

Acknowledgements

I am indebted to the valuable contribution of the early years children at Bickleigh-on-Exe Church of England Primary School, Two Moors Primary School and Great Torrington Bluecoat Church of England Primary School and Early Years Teaching Centre in Devon. I have been delighted by their enthusiasm for mathematics and their questioning and creative approach to their learning. Many people have contributed to this book and I am very grateful for their support and contributions. For this third edition, I would particularly like to thank Sue Copp, Liz Fancourt, Bridget Megson, Janice Harris, Angela Fleming, William Richardson and all my early years colleagues at Bluecoat for their inspirational practice and commitment. Finally, my thanks go to those members of the Devon Mathematics Team who have given me opportunities to develop my own early years practice, and who continue to do so.

How to use this book

This book is organized into nine distinct chapters:

Chapter 1 explores play, problem solving, inclusion and a child's transition from Foundation Stage (5-year-olds) to Year 1 (5–6-year-olds) in Key Stage 1.

Chapter 2 focuses on practical suggestions for creating and using a mathematical environment, both inside and outdoors, including Forest School.

Chapter 3 discusses the importance of mathematical graphics and includes several examples stimulated by playful activity.

Chapter 4 explores counting and using number, giving examples of both focused teaching activities and independent play using the theme of 'Handa's village', based on the popular picture books by Eileen Browne.

Chapter 5 provides ideas for teaching pattern, with practical examples based on the theme of 'clothes'.

Chapter 6 focuses on shape and space, with practical examples related to the theme of 'the street'.

Chapter 7 gives practical ideas about measures using the theme of 'pets'.

Chapter 8 offers support with planning, organizing and assessing independent play, including exemplars of class mathematics session plans along with some photocopiable material.

Chapter 9 details a range of ideas and strategies for involving parents in their child's mathematical development.

A resources section lists storybooks, websites and resources mentioned in the book.

The chapters have a similar layout and are organized to make the book easier for the reader to use. The book contains special features to support the reader, combinations of which will vary slightly from one chapter to another:

'This chapter covers' box is included in each chapter so you can tell if the chapter is likely to meet your needs.

'Principles into practice' boxes give practical examples of the application of good maths subject knowledge and early years pedagogy.

✔ Checklists are included to stimulate thinking about your provision and practice.

'Creative ideas for good practice' boxes suggest imaginative and engaging ways to present practical maths activities and environments.

Case studies and activities illustrate examples of teaching and learning maths through play and in playful contexts.

Mathematical vocabulary is organized and listed in the different areas of mathematics.

ICT boxes suggest ways in which ICT can be used in playful contexts to support the learning of maths.

A Glossary gives an explanation of terms and abbreviations used in each chapter.

Further reading is provided to allow you to explore in greater detail those aspects of the book which can only be touched upon here.

The book is designed to support the reader to develop an appropriate early years mathematical pedagogy by suggesting activities, ideas and resources which promote playful contexts for mathematical learning. It will also enable the reader to develop and consolidate their own mathematical subject knowledge, either directly, or through suggested further reading. This book aims to:

- link creative activities to mathematical learning objectives from the Primary National Strategy and Early Learning Goals of the Foundation Stage, through Key Stage 1 (5–7-year-olds) and into Year 3 (7–8-year-olds) of Key Stage 2 (7–11-year-olds)
- suggest links between maths and other areas of learning
- provide guidance on planning and assessing for class mathematics sessions, for focused group teaching and for independent play based on popular early years themes
- provide practical ideas on how to involve parents in playful mathematics education
- offer practical suggestions to enable a smooth transition from Foundation Stage into Key Stage 1
- support practitioners in implementing mathematical mark making in their settings and schools by including examples of mathematical graphics stimulated by playful activity.

The book is relevant to all early years practitioners, but it is particularly relevant for those working in Reception classes (4–5-year-olds), mixed Reception and Key Stage 1 classes, and all those addressing the transition from Foundation Stage (0–5-year-olds) to Key Stage 1 (5–7-year-olds). It is also relevant for those involved in the transition from Key Stage 1 to Key Stage 2 (7–11-year-olds). The book uses the inclusive term 'practitioner' to refer to the broad range of professionals who work in early years settings and in statutory schooling, while the term 'parent' also includes carers and those with parental responsibility.

Material on the SAGE website

 The photocopiable pages from the book can be found on our website at www.sagepub.co.uk/tucker3e, under 'sample materials'.

1

Play and problem solving

This chapter covers:

- how some theories of play have influenced early years mathematics education
- how play is an appropriate context for problem solving
- creativity and mathematical development
- including all children and families in playful mathematical experiences
- the transition from Foundation Stage (at age 5 years) to KS 1 (5–7 years)
- implications for an appropriate early years mathematics pedagogy.

Why play?

Play is what young children are about, it is what preoccupies them and it can be considered both a mode of behaviour and a state of mind. We understand that play is a natural pursuit for young children, but what we seem less able to understand is how to harness appropriate play pedagogical processes and use them to support mathematical development.

In recent years, it has seemed that a playful approach to learning has been at odds with UK government directives. Teachers of mixed-age early years classes and those teaching Year 1 children (6-year-olds) are aware that the transition from the Early Years Foundation Stage, a distinct phase of play-based education and care from birth to the end of Reception (5-year-olds), to a more subject-specific Year 1 can be disjointed, bewildering and potentially detrimental (Ofsted, 2004). The *Independent Review of Mathematics Teaching in Early Years Settings and Primary Schools* (DCSF, 2008), led by Sir Peter Williams, however, described play as a feature of effective early years pedagogy and stressed the importance of connection making, creative recording and mark making, along with appropriate transition from the Foundation Stage to Year 1. Two further reviews, the *Independent Review of the Primary Curriculum: Final Report* (Rose, 2009) and *Towards a New Primary Curriculum: A Report from the Cambridge Primary Review, Part 2: The Future* (Alexander, 2009), led by Professor Robin Alexander, also regard play as a significant feature of good early years practice. They argue that, far from being trivial, play is an effective and age-appropriate pedagogy and one which concerns itself with *how* children learn, and not merely with *what* they learn. Although play is complex to define, some theories of play have had a particular impact on the teaching of mathematics.

Piaget

Piaget's constructivist theory states that active learning, first-hand experience and motivation are the catalysts for cognitive development. Learning develops through clearly defined ages and stages – a continuum from functional play, through symbolic play to play with rules. Piaget (1958) has not only influenced early years practitioners in their practice of allowing children self-choice, but his work has also been very influential in commercial maths schemes which assume a hierarchical view of mathematical development. This had the effect of advocating 'pre-number' activities, such as matching and sorting before a child could progress to counting and manipulating numbers.

Vygotsky

Vygotsky (1978), unlike Piaget, emphasizes the significance of social interaction, in particular the use of language, which assists learning and development. His social constructivist theory regards social interaction with peers and adults, through which children can make sense of their world and create meaning from shared experiences, as crucial. Learning occurs in the 'zone of proximal development', which represents the difference between what the child actually knows and what the child can learn with the assistance of a 'more knowledgeable other'. Play with others can provide these 'zones' because of the meaningful and motivating social context in which they occur. His influence on mathematics has been to encourage mathematics teaching to be related to the child's own experiences and to encourage talk about mathematics.

Bruner

Like Vygotsky, Bruner (1991) shares social constructivist theories which highlight the significance of interaction with others. Play serves as a vehicle for socialization and its contexts enable children to learn about rules, roles and friendships. The practitioner is proactive in creating interesting and challenging environments and in providing quality interactions, which act as a 'scaffold' for children's learning. He advocates a 'spiral curriculum' where children revisit play materials and activities over time, using them differently at each encounter as their increased development dictates. The structure of the National Numeracy Strategy (DfEE, 1999), with its repeated visits to specific learning objectives each half term, reflected the need for children to revisit ideas and consolidate their learning before moving on to the next stage.

Smilansky and Shefatya

Smilansky and Shefatya (1990) define socio-dramatic play as requiring interaction, communication and cooperation, which allow children to test out ideas and concepts, unlike dramatic play, where the child may play alone. Smilansky and Shefatya suggest that enriched learning comes from the adult working alongside children in their play, or 'play tutoring'. Through play, children can assimilate information and prepare for new situations. By selecting different role-play areas, practitioners can give access to different and appropriate areas of learning. This is a common approach in many early years settings, where the practitioner might establish a cafe or shop in the role-play area to provide a context for developing an understanding of specific mathematical concepts, often those involving the use of money.

Bruce (1991) argues that 'free-flow play' is the purest form of play where play is freely chosen by the child and without the confines of external expectation. During this 'pure' play, children will:

- initiate the activity in a meaningful context
- have control and ownership of the activity by imagining, making decisions and predictions
- experiment with strategies and take risks in this 'safe' context
- show curiosity
- repeat, rehearse and refine observed social behaviours and skills
- seek pleasure from the essence of the activity.

All of these processes, integral to play, are also essential for mathematical thinking and problem solving. Play and mathematics, therefore, seem natural partners, and their combination will allow the child to:

- gain an understanding of the cultural role of mathematics
- have a heightened awareness that mathematics can be useful in the real world
- recognize that mathematical activity can be both sociable and cooperative
- perceive mathematical activity to be enjoyable and purposeful.

In order to fully support mathematical development, playful activity requires adult involvement at some level. Early years curricula in the UK (DfE, 2012; SE, 2007; WAG, 2008) advocate that play which best supports learning is that in which there is a mix of child-initiated and adult-supported play. Indeed, a balance of practitioner-led, practitioner-initiated and child-initiated activity is desirable (Fisher, 2010; Pound, 2008). While practitioner-led activity can ensure the systematic teaching of skills, child-initiated learning, without adult control and dominance, can enable children to become self-regulated learners.

Creativity

There is growing evidence that it is *how* and not *what* a child learns that has greatest impact on their school achievement (Bronson, 2000). The revised EYFS emphasizes *how* children learn by the inclusion of the 'characteristics of effective learning', although it is Dame Tickell's *Independent Report on the Early Years Foundation Stage to Her Majesty's Government* (Tickell, 2011) that provides a more robust discussion about their inclusion. The inclusion of these characteristics – play and exploring, active learning and creating and critical thinking – promote key learning dispositions in the young child such as engagement, motivation and thinking, all of which are necessary for self-regulated learning and also vital for real mathematical enquiry. Arguably, creativity is at the heart of all young children's learning and although difficult to define, can be regarded as comprising of four main aspects: imagination, purpose, originality and value (NACCCE, 1999). When young children are being creative, they:

- are captivated and curious
- will be driven by this curiosity to achieve their goal
- make links in their learning in order to make sense of their activity, refine their thinking and thus give rise to new thinking

- evaluate the process they are engaged in so that they might adapt or refine their task in order to be satisfied with their activity.

Creativity can be encouraged in mathematical play by:

- using open-ended questions and ensuring sustained shared thinking (see 'Prompts and questions for problem solving' below)
- providing open-ended resources (see Chapter 2)
- ensuring time and space for children to explore and extend their enquiry
- allowing children to leave out resources such as wooden blocks, model-making materials, etc., so they can revisit them the following day and develop their thinking further
- ensuring that children have the opportunity to review their work and talk about their thinking using appropriate vocabulary (see 'Review time' below)
- encouraging children to make links between maths and other experiences.

Creating links or connections between areas of learning is widely recognized and advocated as a means of embedding learning and fostering creative thinking (DCSF, 2008; DfE, 2012; DfES, 2006; Rose, 2009). Not only do children need to make sense of the connections between mathematics and other learning, but they should be encouraged to make connections between the aspects of mathematics that bind the mathematical activity itself. Haylock and Cockburn (2013) argue that in order to understand mathematical concepts of number and number operations, children must build up a network of connections between four types of mathematical experience: manipulating concrete objects, symbols, language and pictures. This connection making between images, words and symbols at an early stage will often help children avoid misconceptions at a later stage (Gersten et al., 2005). Play situations can provide the very context in which mathematical vocabulary and symbols can be successfully introduced and practised by the children, enabling them to understand this more easily later on.

Principles into practice

Context: Bakery role play

Prompt: There are five buns on the shelf today. Can you make a record for the baker to show how many have been sold and how many are left?

The children will have opportunities to:

- 'sell' the buns (manipulate concrete objects)
- talk about the experience with peers and adults using the language of number and subtraction (use mathematical language)
- move the buns (create an image or picture)
- record responses using their own graphics or standard notation (use symbols and/or pictures).

Problem solving

Contextualizing mathematical learning and providing for real and purposeful mathematical enquiry lies at the heart of this book. Children are born problem-solvers and innately want to find out 'why?' and 'how?' Problem solving for young children is best provided for in the early years by real situations. Practitioners should be reassured that problem solving does not mean reaching for commercial mathematical investigation packs and worksheets, with their abstract symbols and de-contextualized subject matter. Far better is the frequent facilitation of real problem-solving opportunities. When young children begin formal schooling, they often lose interest and confidence in their mathematical abilities. Their experience of mathematics goes from the meaningful to the abstract very quickly and they can find it difficult to bridge the gap between 'real' and 'school' mathematics (Carruthers and Worthington, 2011; Pound, 2008). The early years practitioner, therefore, needs to provide experiences through which children can make connections and see a purpose in solving problems. Such opportunities will present themselves in everyday routines and experiences such as:

- counting the lunch preferences for the day, finding the most and least popular preference and the difference between the two
- finding how many more (or fewer) children are at school today than yesterday
- making sure there are enough pieces of fruit for everyone at snack time
- calculating the number of resources that have arrived in an order.

These experiences give children opportunities to count both in ones from numbers other than 0 and 1, and in given steps, skills crucial in problem solving (see Chapter 4). Practitioners should also take advantage of these real situations to:

- model mathematical language
- show the process of problem solving itself by allowing children to see them struggling with their own thinking
- provide time, space and open-ended resources
- support children's thinking with the use of sensitive prompts and open questions (see below)
- show that there is not always a 'right' answer and encourage 'draft' thinking
- support children to take risks.

Key to supporting children's ability to solve problems is practitioners having strong subject knowledge (DCSF, 2008), along with a stimulating learning environment (see Chapter 2).

Prompts and questions for problem solving

I wonder what would happen if...?

I wonder why...

Tell me more...

Can you explain your thinking?

How do you know this?

Why do you think that?

How did you know what to do next?

What could you try next?

Do you think that this is the only way…?

How does this make sense?

Do you think this will work?

Why/how do you think this will work?

What might you plan to do next?

How have you been reminded about other learning?

Can you talk about the links you have made in your learning?

Has this given you other ideas?

Is there anything we have talked about that has changed how you will do this next time?

What could you have done to improve your learning?

Real situations are ideal but practitioners can create scenarios where children are 'helping' a fictional character by solving problems and thinking mathematically (see Chapters 4–7).

Inclusion

Inclusive practice promotes the teaching of young children in physical and psychological environments where their abilities are encouraged and where there are high expectations of them as learners. Effective and positive relationships with staff, along with appropriate systems for the sharing of relevant information with families, will enable families to feel welcome and parents will be more likely to engage (see Chapter 9). Children will feel included if they can access all that is offered to them, including space, time and the attention of practitioners. Observation is key as it will:

- inform staff about the current interests of the children, thus enabling provision to be made for them
- monitor which children are accessing which learning contexts
- provide vital information to consider when auditing the learning environment
- provide the opportunity to reflect on whether the resources provided truly reflect the home cultures of the children in attendance.

Regular review of the learning environment is important to ensure that it is truly inclusive for all children and families.

Useful questions when considering inclusion

Do the activities and resources reflect all languages and cultures of the current group of children?

Are the mathematical displays/resources/books accessible and appropriate for the languages and cultures of current children and their families?

Are there areas or activities that are dominated by a particular group? If so, how can this be addressed?

Are there opportunities for children to share their mathematical thinking in different ways such as talking in a group, talking one-to-one, using chosen signing or visual prompts?

Do learning contexts such as play trays or the block area need repositioning to enable greater access by wheelchairs or walking aids?

Are there areas in the environment that are quiet?

Are there areas in the environment that are neutral in colour?

Can all of the children view recorded material on the same colour background?

Do the quiet children have opportunities to share their mathematical thinking in pairs or individually?

Do the very able mathematicians feel that their thinking is challenged and encouraged?

Is there a mix of large- and small-handled tools in the malleable material and painting areas, allowing appropriate access for all children?

Transition

Increased pressure on Year 1 teachers to deliver content and focus on *what* is learnt has undoubtedly contributed to the difficulties often encountered by young children moving from Reception (aged 5) to Y1 (5–6 years) (Ofsted, 2004). Transition should be regarded as a process, to be handled sensitively and not to be regarded as something which is 'done' to the child. Both the *Independent Review of Mathematics Teaching in Early Years Settings and Primary Schools* (DCSF, 2008) and the *Independent Review of the Primary Curriculum: Final Report* (Rose, 2009) suggest that Year 1 teachers should consult the Early Years Foundation Stage Profile passed on to them by the Foundation teachers to inform them about the whole child as well as mathematical attainment. Comments made about their learning dispositions with regard to the characteristics of effective learning will also help teachers to understand and support the child as a self-regulated learner (Stewart, 2011).

Principles into practice

- Continue to prepare a stimulating and inviting environment, both indoors and out-doors. If there is no immediate access outside, ensure there are sessions outside where children play creatively.
- Be mindful of a balance between practitioner-led, practitioner-initiated and child-initiated activity. Try to ensure that children have opportunities for all three over the course of a week.
- Avoid leaving play for Friday afternoons; ensure that there are opportunities during the week and that it becomes embedded in weekly practice.
- Give a high profile to play by ensuring that independent learning time is reviewed and evaluated by the children.
- Provide open-ended resources that lend themselves to exploration and natural problem solving.
- Ensure time and space for high quality play.
- Avoid abrupt changes in routines and pedagogy to enable children to feel secure.
- Allow children to get to know their new environment through regular visits prior to them beginning in Y1.

Implications for an effective early years mathematics pedagogy

As children have a natural propensity to play, it follows that effective provision should capitalize on play as a preferred learning style. Good practice would suggest that practitioners should both harness play as an appropriate learning style and ensure that the children they teach make agreed progress in their mathematical understanding. In order for children to make progress in mathematics, they need to be involved in systematic, focused teaching in small groups where adults are actively teaching (Siraj-Blatchford et al., 2002). This ensures frequent, repeated and appropriate experiences, made all the more effective if the teachers have good subject knowledge and can plan for progression (DCSF, 2008; Gifford, 2008).

Principles into practice

- Ensure a sensitive balance between focused teaching and practitioner-initiated play, practitioner-initiated–child-continued play and child-initiated play (see Glossary).
- Provide opportunities for children to evaluate their activity and discuss their thinking, allowing them to develop their self-efficacy and act as models for self-regulated learning.
- Provide group-focused teaching.
- Plan motivating mathematical activity within playful and meaningful contexts where children can rehearse and refine a range of skills.
- Support children to make links in their learning.
- Ensure that practitioners have strong mathematics subject knowledge and that they can plan for progression.

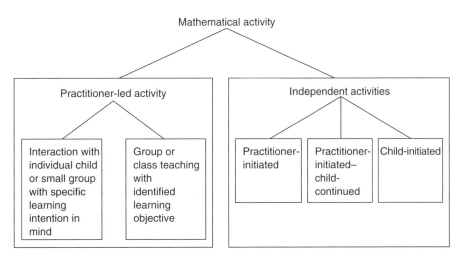

Figure 1.1   Mathematical activity

While the youngest children will be taught maths in integrated sessions, older children in Key Stages 1 and 2 (7–11-year-olds) are generally taught maths in a maths 'lesson'. By incorporating practitioner-led activity (direct teaching) in playful and meaningful contexts, with practitioner-initiated play and child-initiated play into a 'mathematics session', the session can provide a continuum *between* 'work' and 'play' in the following ways:

- Ensure mathematics occurs in a meaningful and stimulating context, such as linking it to the current theme or interests of the children. If the children are enjoying *Handa's Surprise* (see Resources) in their literacy curriculum, then they can 'help' Handa to solve mathematical problems involving fruit and animals (see Chapter 4).
- Link all learning contexts – play trays, role play, small worlds, etc. – by a common theme through which different areas of the curriculum can be accessed which will encourage connection making between experiences (see Chapter 2).
- Include a review time for children to evaluate both their directed and self-initiated activity.

Figure 1.1 summarizes playful mathematical activity, while Figure 1.2 suggests a structure for a playful teaching session for single or mixed-age classes from Reception (4–5-year-olds) to Year 3 (7–8-year-olds).

Review time gives opportunities for the *practitioner* to:

- raise the profile of independent activities
- assess levels of learning and engagement with the characteristics of effective learning
- model language for learning and problem solving
- assist the child to show that there is more than one way to tackle a problem
- give precise feedback about the child's learning processes and thinking.

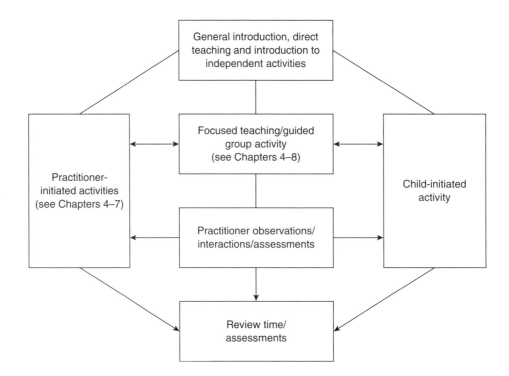

Figure 1.2   Model of an early years mathematics teaching session

Review time gives opportunities for the *child* to:

- practise using language for learning
- present their critical thinking to others
- make connections between their mathematical learning and other experiences and vocalize these to others
- evaluate their thinking and processes of working
- rethink their processes in the light of practitioners' feedback
- perceive themselves as an independent learner and mathematician
- develop their self-efficacy.

Children's language for learning

- I made a mistake, but I corrected my thinking...
- I managed my distractions so I could...
- I made links in my learning...
- I worked well on my own/with others...
- I solved the problem by...
- The questions I asked were...
- I predicted that ... would happen and I found that...

Play, then, is endorsed as an appropriate context for mathematics teaching beyond Foundation Stage; the practice of teachers throughout the primary age range might be greatly informed by a study of early years mathematics pedagogy (Alexander, 2009; DCSF, 2008; Rose, 2009). The ensuing chapters provide examples of teaching mathematics by harnessing children's propensity for play and problem solving through independent play and playful contexts that are characteristic of effective early years pedagogy.

Glossary

Child-initiated: children select their own resources, plan their own activity and pursue their own learning agenda.

EYFS: Early Years Foundation Stage.

KS: Key Stage.

Practitioner-initiated: children follow a task or idea suggested by the practitioner who has a specific learning outcome in mind.

Practitioner-initiated–child-continued: children extend or develop a practitioner-initiated activity to pursue their own learning.

Further reading

Department of Children, Schools and Families (DCSF) (2008) *Independent Review of Mathematics Teaching in Early Years Settings and Primary Schools*. London: DCSF. Useful to read first-hand to identify how play is endorsed.

Fisher, J. (2010) *Moving on to Key Stage 1: Improving Transition from the Early Years Foundation Stage*. Maidenhead: OUP. Clear and accessible, this book describes strategies to support transition from FS to KS1.

Gifford, S. (2008) '"How do you teach nursery children mathematics?" In search of a mathematics pedagogy for the early years', in I. Thompson (ed.) *Teaching and Learning Early Number*, 2nd edition. Maidenhead: OUP. This chapter describes features of an early years mathematics pedagogy for nursery children.

Pound, L. (2008) *Thinking and Learning about Mathematics in the Early Years*. London: Routledge. This book provides the theory underpinning the benefits of a playful and creative approach to early years mathematics

Stewart, N. (2011) *How Children Learn: The Characteristics of Effective Early Learning*. London: The British Association for Early Childhood Education. This very readable book outlines the theory and practice supporting the characteristics of effective learning.

2

Creating and using a mathematical environment

This chapter covers:

- the features of an early years learning environment with examples of how they can promote mathematical development and provide links with other areas of learning
- creative materials and resources
- creating and using mathematical displays
- mathematical activity in the outdoor teaching and learning area and Forest School.

Ethos

The environment plays a crucial role in a child's ability to develop as a self-regulated learner. A learning environment that encourages the child's self-esteem, actively encourages independent learning and positively encourages risk taking will be more successful in supporting a child's agency and efficacy. A successful learning environment is one in which the psychological and physical aspects are afforded equal consideration (see Chapters 1 and 8).

The physical environment

When planning the physical environment, consideration must be given to:

- appropriate resources to inspire and motivate children
- space to enable interaction with peers and a natural flow from one activity to another
- time dedicated to exploring the opportunities they present.

If we wish mathematical activity to occur, we must show evidence of it happening throughout the environment by examining every aspect of continuous provision for mathematical potential and communicating this to the learning community.

Selecting mathematical resources

Natural materials

Often, the best resources tend to be those that are aesthetic, with potential for creative and cross-curricular opportunities such as conkers, acorns and shells. Offered in baskets or boxes, they can be used for many mathematical activities (see Chapters 4 and 5) and can provide meaningful links with other areas of learning:

- science (growth, materials)
- language (stimulating talk about similarities/differences, descriptive language)
- geography (places of origin, the local environment)
- history (will they always stay the same? What will happen if we plant them?)
- creative (using them for printing with, and as a stimulus for observational drawing and painting).

Numerals, number tracks and number lines

Numerals should be prominently and purposefully displayed. Displaying the sign 'Three people can work in the graphics area' alongside the corresponding numeral and array (see Glossary) reinforces the connection between the written word, symbol and array.

Number tracks (with numbered spaces representing natural counting numbers) and number lines (offering possibilities for representing numbers in between natural numbers – see Glossary) should be available to children and can be presented in a variety of playful ways (see Chapter 4).

Creative ideas for good practice

- Supply tactile numeral cards (made out of rough fabric, sandpaper, rope, etc.) and numeral marble runs.
- Provide areas in the environment where children can count interesting and aesthetic objects and label them with the corresponding numeral.
- Provide opportunities for children to see numerals alongside the written word and corresponding array.
- Display numerals in purposeful contexts (on drawers, pots of pencils, construction boxes, posters/signs, etc.).
- Ensure that number lines, both numbered and empty, are readily available for children to refer to and to write on independently.
- Display 'big' numbers, including a hundred square, prominently.
- Make number games readily available.
- Display books about number.

Other mathematical resources

Resources are most successful when they are theme-related and meaningful for the child, however there are a few essential resources that satisfy basic requirements:

- weighing apparatus – bucket balance, scales
- rulers and tape measures
- jugs and scoops of different sizes

- mathematical symbol cards/tiles
- construction kits, including sets of wooden blocks
- sets of 2D and 3D shapes
- calculators
- bead bars/strings
- counting sticks.

Use of space

In the early years learning environment, space should be zoned for different areas of learning. A well-considered environment may allocate space for the following learning contexts:

- play trays
- small worlds
- role play
- graphics area
- construction area
- reading and listening area
- ICT
- modelling/malleable materials and painting area
- 'washing line'.

Not only can these learning contexts provide excellent, creative mathematical learning opportunities (see Chapters 4–7), they can also act as 'meeting places' where children can discuss ideas, collaborate, solve problems and make important connections between maths and other learning. Pound (2008) argues that offering such opportunities 'is to be welcomed because it highlights the links between mathematics and other aspects of life and learning'. Table 2.1 summarizes mathematical opportunities in these learning contexts.

Displays

The most successful displays are of current investigations which reflect the children's thinking. It is important to display children's own mathematical graphics (see Chapter 3) as this raises the profile of the children's own marks and, by implication, their thinking and problem solving. Children's graphics that communicate mathematical symbols also act to provide an 'environmental model for children' (Carruthers and Worthington, 2011).

Principles into practice

- Provide a display board at child height specifically for children's mathematical graphics. This allows children to select and display their own work, thus giving them ownership of the process.
- Allow children to 'publish' their own booklets about mathematical concepts and display these alongside real books about the same maths theme.
- Where the nature of the recorded work is not immediately accessible to others, display explanations of the intended communication alongside.

Table 2.1   Learning contexts

Learning context	Mathematical features	Resources
Play trays	Offers problem solving involving counting, sorting, pattern making, mathematical operations, shape and measures. (See Table 2.2 for examples of activities and links with other areas of the curriculum.)	• acorns • buttons • conkers • corn • cornflour and water ('gloop') • dog biscuits • fir/pine cones • gravel • leaves • pasta (dried) • paste (water and flour, coloured) • porridge oats • potting compost • sawdust • spaghetti (cooked, coloured, sprinkled in oil) • straw • twigs/bark • wood shavings • wood • wool
Small-world dramas	The 'bird's eye' view of play stimulates the purposeful use of positional and directional language.	• blue, green, brown, grey fabric/hessian for fields, roads, seas, rivers, etc. • plastic/wooden blocks placed beneath the fabric to create undulating landscapes • natural materials: pine cones; driftwood; bark, to create shelters/enclosures/fencing • small animals, play people, houses, vehicles
Role play	Structured role play – café, vets' surgery, travel agents, etc. encourage the writing of lists, bills and receipts and the use of money to buy items and give change. (See Table 2.3 for mathematical opportunities in role play.)	• address/appointment books and cards • bucket balance • calendars and diaries • calculator • cash till • clocks (digital and analogue with clear numerals) • coins and credit cards • dials • dressing-up clothes • forms and notebooks • jugs/containers (of different sizes) • numeral cards (for numbering patients' beds in the hospital etc.) • price tags • recipes • stamps • tape measures • ICT equipment (decommissioned), e.g. telephones, keyboard, laptop, scanner, monitor, etc.
	Unstructured role play – young children, aged 3–5, benefit most from unstructured role play using open-ended resources (see Further reading). This facilitates emerging social and problem-solving skills. Observations may reveal whether the children are using mathematical vocabulary with understanding and their preferred schemas.	• plain tabards • scarves/lengths of fabric • large wooden blocks/crates/wooden frames for den making • cardboard tubes and boxes of varying sizes • writing materials • counting collections (see Chapter 4) • 'treasure' (old jewellery/glass beads) • bunches of keys • bowls, plates, cups, tankards in different materials

(Continued)

Table 2.1   (Continued)

Learning context	Mathematical features	Resources
Graphics area	A dedicated 'work station' for writing and drawing and combines literacy and mathematical graphics. It can be provided for in a tool box, allowing the resources to be carried from one space to another as needed.	• paper of varying colour, shapes and sizes (including squared paper) • pencils and coloured pens • scissors • glue sticks • stapler • sellotape • ready-made booklets of differing sizes • number lines (including empty number lines) • sheets of large numerals (suitable for cutting out) • sheets of mathematical vocabulary (suitable for cutting out) • plastic 2D shapes (for drawing around) • ruler
Construction area	Offers exploration of individual shapes and the spatial relationship between them. Encourages strategies for using blocks to record children's mathematical thinking and problem solving.	• wooden blocks • commercial kits • clearly labelled boxes with words and pictures to help with tidying and storing • challenge cards, e.g. 'can you …?' and prompt cards, e.g. 'the queen built a large castle …' • writing materials for children to record responses • small-world animals and people for children to extend their play
Reading and listening areas	Supports and extends mathematical vocabulary.	See Resources
ICT	Supports all aspects of maths. There are some specific examples later in the book which are referenced here.	• Cameras (Chapter 4) • IWB (Chapter 4) • Visualizers (Chapter 6) • Digital microscope (Chapter 5) • Talking boxes (Chapter 4) • Programmable toys (Chapter 6) • Video conferencing (Chapter 7) • SMART interactive table (Chapter 5) • ipad • laptops
Malleable materials and painting area	Modelling dough used to construct and deconstruct shapes; explore length; form numerals. Paint – paint numerals and explore repeating patterns, number, shape, space and position.	• modelling dough • paint • clay tools • theme-related objects
Washing line	Offers opportunities to sequence numerals and measures (including big pictures of coins) and construct repeating patterns along its length.	• laminated numeral cards • theme-related pictures

Table 2.2 Mathematical play tray activities

Context for play and suggested resources	Concept/Skill	Examples of mathematical activity	Links with other areas of learning
Planting Potting compost; butter beans; plant pots (of different sizes); trowels	• estimating how many • counting • using vocabulary of number and capacity • exploring pouring and filling • comparing and ordering capacities	• filling and emptying plant pots • planting beans	• science – growth, materials • literacy – *Jasper's Beanstalk* by Nick Butterworth and Mick Inkpen
Dinosaur swamp Green paste (water, flour, green food colouring); smooth twigs/driftwood; pebbles; plastic dinosaurs of different sizes	• ordering by size • counting • using vocabulary of number • partitioning • making a sequence or pattern • counting	• lining up dinosaurs in order of size • constructing enclosures for the dinosaurs • lining up minibeasts in a sequence or pattern	• science – materials, changing materials • literacy – *Bumpus Jumpus Dinosaurumpus* by Tony Mitton and Guy Parker-Rees • science – materials • geography – natural materials from the local environment
In the wood Twigs; leaves; conkers; acorns; pieces of bark; plastic minibeasts	• making fair shares	• making homes for equal numbers of minibeasts	• literacy – *Ladybird, Ladybird* by Ruth Brown; *The Gruffalo* by Julia Donaldson and Axel Scheffler
Goldilocks Mugs of 'milk' for the three bears (water with a little white powder or liquid paint); 3 cups of different sizes; jugs	• exploring pouring and filling • estimating how much • comparing and ordering capacities	• filling and emptying cups of 'milk'	• science – changing materials • literacy – *Goldilocks and the Three Bears* (traditional)
Clothes Buttons of different shapes, colours and sizes; 'clothes', 'boots', 'shoes' (card outlines of trousers, dresses, boots, etc. covered in fabric)	• making a sequence or pattern • sorting • counting • using language of number • exploring and comparing areas	• selecting buttons to lie in a line on the front of the 'garment' • covering 'clothes' in buttons	• geography – clothes suitable for different weathers • art/design – selecting colour/style • literacy – *Jamaica and Brianna* by Juanita Havill and Anne Sibley O'Brien
Designing a garden Wet sand; dried/artificial flowers; pebbles; sticks; shells	• making a sequence or pattern • exploring properties of 2D shapes • using vocabulary of shape and position	• laying out pebbles, flowers, shells, etc. in a sequence or pattern • sculpting shapes	• science – materials • art – sculpture • literacy – *Mary, Mary Quite Contrary* (traditional); *The Sand Horse* by Ann Turnbull and Michael Foreman

(Continued)

Table 2.2 (Continued)

Context for play and suggested resources	Concept/Skill	Examples of mathematical activity	Links with other areas of learning
Jungle swamp 'Swamp' (green food colouring in water); pebbles; driftwood/twigs; plastic snakes and lizards of different lengths	• comparing and ordering by length • counting • using language of number and measurement • making a sequence or pattern	• arranging creatures in order of length • laying out creatures in a sequence or pattern	• science – materials • geography – habitats • literacy – *The Enormous Crocodile* by Roald Dahl and Quentin Blake
On the farm Grain; small hessian sacks of different sizes; scoops	• exploring pouring and filling • estimating how many • counting • using language of number and capacity • comparing and ordering capacities	• filling and emptying sacks with grain	• science – materials, food • literacy – *Rosie's Walk* by Pat Hutchins
In the pet shop Dog biscuits (of different shapes and colours); thick paper bags; scoops	• sorting • making a sequence or pattern • counting • exploring properties of 2D shapes • exploring pouring and filling • estimating how many • using language of number and capacity	• selecting biscuits to put into bags • laying out biscuits in a sequence or pattern • filling and emptying bags	• science – food • literacy – *The Pet Shop* by Allan Ahlberg and Andre Amstutz; *A Bit More Bert* by Allan Ahlberg and Raymond Briggs
Noah's Ark 'Sea' (blue food colouring in water); large plastic boat; twigs/driftwood; leaves/ greenery; pairs of plastic animals; play people	• sorting • making a sequence/pattern • counting in 1s and 2s • partitioning	• matching animals • laying out animals in a sequence or pattern • marching animals into the ark	• literacy/KE – *Noah's Ark* (traditional) • science – materials
Fishing game Numbered laminated card fish with paper-clip attachments; fishing rods (dowelling, string with magnet)	• counting • numeral recognition • addition by counting on	• counting fish caught • reading numeral on fish • devising simple games	• science – magnets • literacy – *The Mousehole Cat* by Antonia Barber and Nicola Bayley
Animal journey 'Lake' (card covered in silver paper); stones; twigs; greenery; plastic animals (mice, frogs, butterflies, lizards, crickets, etc.); play people	• sorting • counting • making a sequence or pattern • partitioning • making fair shares	• putting animals into like groups • laying out animals in a sequence or pattern • making enclosures for animals	• science – materials • geography – habitats, Africa • literacy – *Handa's Hen* and *Handa's Surprise* by Eileen Browne

Table 2.3 Mathematical opportunities in role play

Concept/Skill	Possible mathematical activities in the Flower Shop	Possible mathematical activities in the Health Centre	Possible mathematical activities in the Pirates' Voyage
Reading/Writing numerals	<ul><li>using cash till/telephone/calendar/credit cards</li><li>making price tags</li><li>filling in order forms</li><li>writing addresses and telephone numbers</li><li>writing cheques</li><li>writing opening/closing times</li><li>labelling displays</li></ul>	<ul><li>writing/reading appointment cards</li><li>using calendar/telephone</li><li>writing in/reading appointment book</li><li>writing prescriptions</li><li>writing addresses</li><li>using waiting number tags</li></ul>	<ul><li>reading numerals on doubloons</li><li>recording times/dates/items of treasure found in logbook</li><li>using/making maps</li></ul>
Counting	<ul><li>flowers in 1s, 2s, 5s, 10s</li><li>message cards in packs of 10</li><li>rolls of ribbons</li><li>number of plant pots</li></ul>	<ul><li>number of patients</li><li>appointment cards in 1s, 2s, 5s, 10s</li><li>prescription bundles</li></ul>	<ul><li>counting biscuits/rations</li><li>treasure</li><li>doubloons in 1s and bags of 10s</li></ul>
Ordering	<ul><li>items on the shelf in price order</li><li>plant pots by size</li><li>flowers by stem length</li></ul>	<ul><li>patients in the queue</li><li>position in queue number tags</li></ul>	<ul><li>telescopes by length</li><li>bags of treasure by weight</li></ul>
Sorting	<ul><li>ribbon by colour/length</li><li>flowers by colour</li><li>plant pots by size</li><li>flowers by stem length</li><li>coins in cash till</li></ul>	<ul><li>bandages, plasters, medicine bottles</li></ul>	<ul><li>jewels/treasure/doubloons</li></ul>
Mathematical operations	<ul><li>calculating prices</li><li>giving change</li><li>calculating total number of flowers/messages</li><li>cards by counting in 2s, 5s, 10s</li></ul>	<ul><li>calculating the total number of appointment cards by counting in 10s</li></ul>	<ul><li>sharing jewels/doubloons among the crew</li><li>finding the total amount of doubloons</li></ul>
Pattern	<ul><li>flowers by colour for window display</li><li>pots and flowers for display</li></ul>		<ul><li>hanging small coloured flags (bunting) in a pattern</li></ul>

(Continued)

Table 2.3 (Continued)

Concept/Skill	Possible mathematical activities in the Flower Shop	Possible mathematical activities in the Health Centre	Possible mathematical activities in the Pirates' Voyage
Weighing	• amount of flower bulbs		• estimating/comparing weight of treasure
Measuring length	• estimating/measuring length of ribbon • estimating/measuring length of flower stems	• estimating/measuring length of bandages	• estimating/measuring length of telescopes/bunting
Time	• using clock • making/displaying opening and closing time signs • recording times of deliveries	• using clock • giving appointment times • displaying opening/closing times • time each patient's appointment	• recording dates in logbook
Shape and space	• wrapping flowers in differently shaped paper/cellophane	• applying bandages	• making small flags • drawing picture maps
Capacity	• filling paper bags with flower bulbs	• filling boxes with rolls of bandages	• filling bags/boxes with treasure
Using money	• making amounts • giving change		• using doubloons as currency

Good mathematics displays need to be interactive and a mix of 2D and 3D displays, taking a variety of forms:

- data displaying the contents of the snack basket or lunch preferences
- wall displays involving counting or pattern that can be discussed and changed daily (see Chapter 5)
- 3D displays of objects for children to manipulate, count, order by specific criteria or arrange in a pattern (see Chapter 4)
- photographs of mathematical activities in role-play situations, or the outside environment, accompanied by written descriptions or documentation
- themed displays showing connections between mathematics and other areas of learning.

Creative ideas for good practice

- Use children's theme-related paintings for pattern making, such as different sized leaves on a giant beanstalk, garments on a washing line or toy vehicles in a traffic jam.
- During a theme about the garden centre, for example, display baskets of large seeds, small plastic wallets and mathematical questions alongside. By counting and bagging the seeds in 10s, a quick and effective display can be made to show what 100 actually looks like.
- Put numerals on objects such as cardboard lighthouses made during technology sessions to stimulate mathematical opportunities in small-world play (see Photo 2.1).
- Encourage children to record their mathematical graphics or lunch choices in the form of a pictogram (see Glossary) on an IWB using a virtual pen to share with parents as they come into the setting on a morning (see Chapter 4).

Display checklist ✓

- Are the children involved in making the display?
- If the display is of completed work, what questions need to be displayed alongside to encourage reflection and talk?
- What information/types of questions need to be displayed to enable parents/carers and others to understand and value the child's work?
- Are all aspects of mathematics displayed over the course of a term?
- What resources or questions could be added to displays from other curriculum areas to help create a mathematical learning environment?

The outside environment

Learning outdoors has long been considered an important aspect of early years education; Margaret Macmillan, Friedrich Froebel and Susan Isaacs have all advocated the benefits of outdoor learning. In recent years, there seems to have been a revival of outdoor learning and the EYFS endorses this as good practice; many settings are now offering outdoor classrooms and Forest School education. The provision of outdoor learning is considerably more than a consideration of resourcing and

Photo 2.1 Including numerals and simple artefacts in this technology display stimulates small-world play with a mathematical content

deployment of staff; indeed Forest School education has a specific pedagogy. It is not the place of this book to discuss the pedagogical principles here (see Further reading) but merely to suggest how to provide for an environment that encourages and supports young children's mathematical development in playful contexts. Pratt (2011) argues that in order for children to become effective mathematicians they should develop a 'mathematical disposition'. This, he suggests, can be supported by the doing of maths outdoors, enabling children to develop an awareness that maths is all around them, allowing them to make connections in their learning and experience natural materials in situ. Knight (2011) suggests that children will be more creative outdoors where they have freedom to be 'innovative, flexible and adaptable' and that this environment will stimulate creative mathematical thinking. To summarize, exploring mathematics outdoors is beneficial as it will:

- offer a sense of freedom without the 'constraints' of the indoor environment
- encourage a 'mathematical disposition' and enable children to make useful links in their learning
- be memorable in that it offers mathematical pursuits in a context not normally associated with mathematical learning
- encourage exploration and risk taking
- support emotional well-being
- contribute to the child's self-image of themselves as a 'mathematician'.

It is important, however, to consider the outdoor and indoor environments as complementary spaces that are linked by their capacity to support children's interests and extend their learning. Some children will of course prefer one environment to the other because of the different opportunities and atmospheres each affords. Adults should be clear about their role outdoors: are adults there to lead guided work or to support children's own initiated activity? Indeed, Forest School activities would not be true to their principles if they were heavily practitioner-directed.

There are several types of outdoor provision and Bilton (2010) offers definitions. Considered here are two broad types: (1) the dedicated outside teaching and learning area – an enclosed, supervised outdoor space, where children will have free-flow access between indoors and outdoors, and (2) the Forest School experience.

Outdoor teaching and learning area

This outside space should support the seven areas of learning in the EYFS which are Communicating and language (CL); Physical development (PD); Personal, social and emotional development (PSED); Literacy (L); Mathematics (M); Understanding the world (UW) and Expressive arts and design (EAD). These areas may more easily be planned and provided for if the outdoor area can be organized into zones that complement one another. When considering provision in this space practitioners should consider the following points:

- ensure continuity of management strategies and ethos between inside and outside
- give equal status to the teaching and learning of mathematics in each environment
- plan to ensure meaningful links between inside and outside themes and learning areas
- plan for appropriate access for all children
- provide quality and appropriate resources
- provide dedicated time and space for mathematical activity
- allow free-flow access between the environments where this is physically possible, and where it is not, ensuring that children have good 'chunks' of the day outside
- plan for assessment and evaluation of mathematics inside and outside.

Principles into practice

During a theme on 'clothes', practitioners might plan:

- launderette role play inside, while outside there may be washing lines, streets of clothes shops built out of blocks, ride-on 'delivery vans' delivering 'dry-cleaning', numbered parking spaces, etc.
- that all practitioners working in the team spend time in both environments, ensuring that children do not perceive practitioners as 'the inside one' or 'the outside one'
- that a balance of focused teaching and independent activity is carried out and assessed in each environment
- to display photographs of mathematical activities and recorded work from both environments.

Table 2.4 Mathematical opportunities outside

Area of learning	Features stimulating mathematical activity
Expressive arts and design	(In addition to role-play resources list) • dressing-up clothes on numbered hangers • signposts • road signs
Understanding the world (construction)	• numbered and labelled construction kits/trolleys • wooden planks/bamboo/tubing/guttering of different lengths and widths • diggers/ride-on toys with number plates • road signs illustrating speeds, distances • frames to encourage tessellating unit blocks, such as a plywood 'roof' with rim
(science)	• laminated labels indicating dates of planting/order of planting – 1st, 2nd, 3rd • equipment, including clipboard, for measurement and recording • tubs/flower pots of graduated size • buckets/watering cans of different capacities • funnels of graduated size • laminated questions such as, 'How many ladybirds can you find today?' • play tray activities • a selection of natural materials presented in such a way as to encourage pattern making
(ICT)	• a camera for filming the mathematical activity • control technology toys to program movement around a course made by wooden blocks etc. • recording equipment to record 'mathematical stories'/measurements made in the garden area etc. • Apple TV
Physical development (large scale)	• numbered ladders and A-frames • equipment laid out in an identifiable sequence or pattern, straight or curved lines • tunnels of different lengths
(small scale)	• equipment stored in bags of 2s, 5s, 10s • numbered cones • access to games/targets that encourage numeral recognition/shape recognition/counting • sand timers to mark start/stop for specific games
Maths/communication and language/Literacy	• number mat • books depicting number and mathematical skills and concepts (see Resources) • mathematical rhymes and story CDs/recordings

Table 2.4 suggests how mathematical opportunities can be planned for in the outdoor teaching and learning area.

Resources that support outdoor mathematical development include:

• big number tiles, digit cards and numbered cones
• cones numbered in multiples of 10s – this is particularly useful if the children are engaged in counting large numbers of interesting leaves or stones that they have collected
• permanent ground markings, such as parking spaces, number lines, number snakes and decision trees. If these are left unnumbered, the children can number them themselves using number cones or tiles
• containers that can be labelled and numbered to provide further opportunities for sorting, counting and numeral recognition. These also create links with inside management (Bilton, 2010)
• a portable graphics area, such as a tool box containing mark-making resources, number lines, digit cards, etc.

Table 2.5 Mathematical activities for Sukkot

Activity	Environment	Opportunities for mathematics
Making biscuits for a 'celebratory' meal. Counting 10 biscuits on each plate	Inside	• weighing ingredients • counting in 1s and groups of 10s • measuring capacity • using related mathematics vocabulary
Collecting natural materials (branches, ivy, leaves) for roof construction	Outside	• discussion of shapes and sizes of leaves • comparison of lengths of leaves and branches • discussion of patterns on leaves • use of mathematical vocabulary
Construction of three-sided structure for sukkah using hollow wooden blocks/crates	Outside	• discussion of optimum size and position • tessellation of blocks and exploration of properties of shapes • measurement of height, depth, width • exploration of symmetry • problem solving – will it be big enough for us?
Decorating sukkah by constructing paper chains and making celebratory posters	Outside or inside	• constructing paper chains in a colour pattern, such as blue, red, blue, red • incorporating 2D shapes and numerals into posters
Pouring drinks for a celebratory meal	Inside or outside	• using mathematical vocabulary of volume and capacity • measuring capacity • counting • equal shares
Developing role play using a celebratory meal and previous discussions about Sukkot as a stimulus	Outside	• sharing biscuits and drinks fairly • 'reading' mathematical posters • addressing/reading invitations to a celebratory meal • counting/setting places for a celebratory meal

Table 2.5 illustrates how natural links between the inside and outside environments can be used effectively in the teaching and learning of mathematics in mixed-age classes. It illustrates mathematical opportunities based on the Jewish festival Sukkot (see Glossary).

Forest School

Forest School education provides children with a 'wild' context where they are presented with risks and challenges. It is underpinned by truly inclusive principles with great emphasis on personal, social and emotional development, and with an overriding aim to support children in understanding their own capabilities and relationships within their group in the 'forest' environment. The wild and natural environment offered by Forest School encourages a creative freedom that the indoor environment cannot and it is here where children are more likely to be innovative (Knight, 2011). Activity undertaken in Forest School by young children may not necessarily sit comfortably in one curriculum area, but may fluctuate between several. Children will develop their own line of enquiry to satisfy their curiosity and will often find themselves deeply involved in purposeful mathematical investigations. The practitioner's skilful observation will identify mathematical activity when it occurs and sensitive prompts and open questioning can support the creative mathematics as it unfolds. This is illustrated in the following case studies.

Case study: Measuring 'worms' – Foundation Stage (Reception) (4–5 years)

The Reception children prepared for their first Forest School session. The Forest School practitioners' primary aims for the session were to introduce health and safety routines for this and all future sessions, and to set a simple, achievable task enabling all children to succeed. In order to encourage the children to explore the site safely and to facilitate their careful observation, the Forest School practitioners had placed string 'worms' around a designated area. The children were invited to look for the 'worms' and gather up what they found. Working alone, or with others, they began to investigate this new environment and seek out their 'worms'. This simple task gave the practitioners the opportunity to observe the children as they interacted with the environment and with one another. Two girls worked together and, satisfied with their 'worm' collection, sat on a log and lay their discoveries in a line along the log's length. They spontaneously began to compare the worms' lengths, picking up individual worms and laying them alongside others as they discussed their observations and conclusions. The children were highly involved in their exploration, spending an extended period of time comparing the 'worms' using mathematical language. The unobtrusive observation by a practitioner enabled her to notice that:

- the girls were able to develop their self-initiated mathematical enquiry in a collaborative and playful context
- both girls displayed an understanding of comparison as a means of measuring length
- the girls used such language as 'longest', 'shortest', 'shorter than', 'longer than', 'biggest', 'smallest' with understanding
- the girls may be displaying signs of a trajectory schema which could be confirmed by further observations, both indoors and out, and, if confirmed, could then be planned for and extended.

Case study: Estimating numbers and measures – Years 1 and 2 (6 and 7 years)

The children had spent the morning whittling willow to make puppets. They had gathered together for their drink and snack and were enjoying this social time. Two boys spontaneously began to gather sticks around them. One of the boys began to hammer a stick into a small earthy area beside him. The second boy joined him, enquiring how many sticks they might need to fill this space. The boys began to work collaboratively and as they worked they talked continuously about the number of sticks they would need to completely fill the space. As she observed the boys' activity, it became clear to the Forest School practitioner that the boys had devised their own rule for the way in which the sticks should be hammered into the ground. The boys had decided that they must place each stick exactly the same distance from the next one and did so without the use of any uniform unit to measure, merely estimating by sight. As they continued to hammer the sticks, they revised their earlier estimates of the number of sticks needed, now estimating in multiples of 10. Finally, their work was complete. They had hammered 35 sticks and were confident that the sticks were placed at equal intervals. The boys were eager to talk about their activity with the other children and this gave the Forest

School practitioner the opportunity to ask the children how they were certain that the sticks were placed equal distances apart. This prompted discussion in the group about the use of standard units of measurement. Without a standard measure to hand, some children suggested using a short stick as a unit of measurement. The boys were happy to adopt this uniform non-standard measure and, using a short stick, readjusted some of their arrangement, ensuring that it was accurate. While some children in the group began to count the sticks in ones, other children began counting in twos. This spontaneous, playful activity of gathering and hammering sticks gave rise to a lively discussion about the use and application of mathematics and provided a real and immediate context for exploring estimation, uniform measures and counting in different units.

Photo 2.2   Children estimating equal distances between sticks

Creative ideas for good practice

- Encourage a positive ethos in the learning environment which enables children to perceive themselves as competent and enthusiastic mathematicians.
- Provide interactive displays, labels and signs that support mathematical thinking and activity.
- Establish creative, well-planned contexts for play which promote the use of mathematical vocabulary and for which there are clearly identified learning intentions.
- Ensure all areas of the learning environment provide rich mathematical opportunities in order to facilitate good quality child-initiated mathematical learning.
- Provide dedicated time and space for children to use the learning environment for both practitioner-initiated and child-initiated play, and use the environment to show how these are valued.
- Give equal status to the teaching and learning of mathematics in both outside and inside environments.

Glossary

Array: an ordered collection of objects or numbers, often presented in rows or columns.

ICT: information and communication technology.

IWB: interactive whiteboard.

Natural numbers: the number 1 and any other number derived by adding 1 to it repeatedly.

Ordinal: a number denoting the perdition in a sequence, such as 1st, 2nd, 3rd, etc.

Pictogram: a visual representation of data using pictures to denote the nature of the information it represents.

Schema: repeated patterns of behaviour in young children.

Sukkot: a Jewish autumn festival during which families build a three-sided shelter (sukkah) with a roof made of branches and greenery in their garden. It reminds them of the Jews' journey from Egypt to Israel.

Further reading

Bilton, H. (2010) *Outdoor Learning in the Early Years: Management and Innovation*, 3rd edition. Abingdon: Routledge. This comprehensive book outlines the history of outdoor learning and offers practical advice on planning and provision.

Bruce, T. (ed.) (2012) *Early Childhood Practice: Froebel Today*. London: Sage Publications. Based on Froebelian principles, the emphasis of this book is on the education of the whole child and includes chapters on learning outdoors.

Knight, S. (2013) *Forest School and Outdoor Learning in the Early Years*, 2nd edition. London: Sage Publications. The principles and benefits of Forest School education in the early years are presented here, along with guidance on planning and developing Forest School provision.

Parton, G. (2012) *Belair: Early Years – ICT: Ages 3–5*. Glasgow: Collins Educational. This text contains lots of practical ideas for activities and displays using a variety of ICT equipment in the learning environment.

Rogers, S. and Evans, J. (2008) *Inside Role Play in Early Childhood Education*. London: Routledge. This book explores how a child's involvement in role play, and particularly unstructured role play, helps develop their social skills and dispositions for learning and problem solving consistent with those required by the emerging mathematician.

Waite, S. (ed.) (2011) *Children Learning Outside the Classroom: From Birth to Eleven*. London: Sage Publications. This edited book explores why learning beyond the classroom is important, giving examples which provide links between theory and practice.

White, J. (ed.) (2011) *Outdoor Provision in the Early Years*. London: Sage Publications. This is a very accessible book with clearly signposted prompts and ideas to help the reader understand, plan and develop a range of outdoor learning experiences.

3

Creative recording and mathematical graphics

This chapter covers:

- the meaning of mathematical graphicacy
- ways to stimulate and support mathematical graphics through play
- examples of mathematical graphics stimulated by play from the Foundation Stage (birth to 5 years) to Year 2 (6–7 years).

The worksheet or creative recording?

By their very nature, workbooks and sheets, often being curricular and objective driven, cannot begin with what individual children know, or indeed what interests them. They rarely inspire creativity, nor do they offer opportunities for children to make meaningful links between aspects of their learning. The worksheet demands that every child should respond in the same way, inhibiting creativity. Children's own mathematical mark making, away from the constraints of the worksheet, affords children the creative freedom to explore, invent strategies and solve problems that make sense to them. The EYFS and the *Independent Review of Mathematics Teaching in Early Years Settings and Primary Schools* (DCSF, 2008) fully support children's own mathematical mark making, suggesting practitioners should value children's own mathematical graphic and practical explorations. Merely recording what has been done following a mathematical activity, however, has little mathematical value as this does not support thinking but merely acts as a record of what has been done. Carruthers and Worthington (2011) argue that there is a significant difference between recording maths and mathematical graphicacy.

What is mathematical graphicacy?

Carruthers and Worthington (2011) argue against the term 'mark making' when considering a child's graphical response to problem solving. They suggest 'mark making' is a generic term that ignores the significance of the child's personal drawings and signs children may use when they are expressing their mathematical thinking. Graphicacy, they argue, emphasizes the significance of all pictorial representations acting as 'mental methods on paper', with its very purpose being to solve mathematical problems and represent deep-level mathematical thinking. These inventive notations may be marks, symbols and drawings on paper, with pen, paint or chalk, but they may also be creative arrangements made out of blocks, pine cones and many assorted objects. In their non-hierarchical taxonomy of mathematical graphics, Carruthers and Worthington (2011) outline 'dimensions' through which children will move as their mathematical graphics develop from birth to 8 years and above. These can be summarized as:

- explorations with marks and symbols
- early written numerals
- numerals as labels
- representing quantities
- children's own methods for calculations.

The 'dimensions' provide a window for practitioners through which they can begin to understand children's mathematical graphics and how best to support them.

Development and examples

Explorations with marks

Young children's mark making may involve repeated behaviours such as the manipulation and arrangement of everyday objects, and scribbling with pens, chalk and other writing media. Athey (1990) describes these repeated patterns of behaviour as 'schemas' and claims that they often suggest mathematical thought and investigation. Through these repeated behaviours, such as pouring and filling or laying objects in straight lines, children are making discoveries about capacity, volume, shape, length, perimeter and repeating pattern (see Chapter 9). As well as making marks by using physical objects in arrangements, young children are often seen 'scribbling' with pens or paint. On closer observation, these scribbles often hold significant meaning for the child. Only on discussion with the child and an understanding of the context in which the marks are made, are their mathematical significance revealed.

Freya's number line

Context: Nursery (3 and 4 years)

Freya, along with a small group of children, spontaneously began to play with a large, roll-out number line from 0 to 10. The children laid it out and took it in turns to jump along, counting jumps as they did so. They repeated this for several minutes and as the play began to break down, their practitioner suggested that they might like to make their own number line. With activity now refocused, the children collected paper and pens and, working on the floor, began to write their own number line. Freya worked silently at her number line for about 15 minutes (Figure 3.1).

The teacher made the following notes on discussion with the child:

- Freya described the top line as 'numbers'. She demonstrated that she understands the idea of a number line as a continuous line of numerals as labels and which here represent counting.

- The next two lines are repeating patterns. 'H, F, H, F' represents 'Holly, Freya, Holly, Freya' followed by a 'big dot, little dot' pattern. She shows a sound understanding of simple, repeating pattern and she is beginning to make links between patterns and the number line.
- The last line is a '4 number line'. Freya is 4 years old and therefore this number is significant to her.
- Freya's last line is a 'beach number line with shells and sea'. As her number line develops, she continues to make connections with other experiences involving lines, counting and patterns.

Next steps:

- Ensure that Freya has plenty of opportunities to use and make a variety of number lines as they have clearly captured her interest.
- Support the understanding of the connections Freya is beginning to make between pattern and the number line, for example by matching Numicon® plates (see Chapter 4) to numerals along the number line. This will also allow her to see the connections between the ordinal and cardinal aspects of number.

Early written numerals

Children's early mathematical graphics may reflect a mix of letters and numerals, as seen in Freya's number line (Figure 3.1). Occasionally, they may use their own numeral system where they ascribe a number to the same mark consistently over a period of time. Similarly, they may make significant marks to which they later ascribe a numeral.

Figure 3.1   Freya's number line

Numerals as labels

Once children have experienced writing numerals as an integral part of their play, such as in their role play, and have become more confident with their use, they may then begin to use numerals as labels. Their drawings might, for example, show a birthday cake with a '3' on it, thus illustrating a numeral that is personal to them. This gives us a window into how they are making sense of their world and the connections they are making between what they observe and what they do.

Charlotte's houses

Context: Reception class (4 and 5 years)

Following discussion about houses and subsequent domestic role play, Charlotte went to the graphics area. Her teacher had provided some house-shaped zigzag books that day and Charlotte began creating her 'street' (Figure 3.2).

Figure 3.2 Charlotte's houses

The teacher made the following notes on discussion with the child:

- Charlotte's own house is number 11 and so she decided she would write this on one of her houses. She described 4 as her 'favourite number' and decided she would put it on the last house 'because I like 4'.
- Charlotte can write and recognize 11 and 4.

- Charlotte understands that numerals seen in the environment have significance and that she is beginning to understand the broad function of numbers.
- Charlotte understands that numbers of personal significance can be committed to paper as a numerical label.

Next steps:

- Give Charlotte a range of opportunities to write numerals and to notice when her graphics reflect an understanding of the ordinal nature of number.

Representing quantities

Young children are often fascinated by big numbers, revelling in the thought that a number can not only exceed their own age, but that they can go on and on. While they may yet be unable to write numerals that accurately represent either a counted large quantity, or an estimate of one, they can confidently make marks to represent their thoughts of the 'bigness' of numbers.

Dillon's pancakes

Context: Nursery class (3 and 4 years) in a primary school

On Shrove Tuesday, Dillon had listened to *The Story of Little Babaji* by Helen Bannerman (see Resources) and was interested in the large number of pancakes made and eaten at the end of the story. Dillon joined a group of children who were role playing making and eating pancakes. He spontaneously collected some circular paper from the graphics area and drew circle shapes all over it (Figure 3.3).

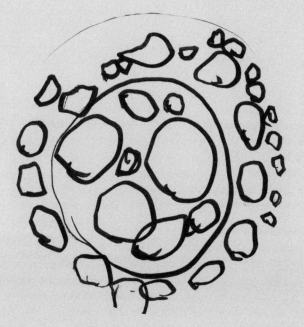

Figure 3.3 Dillon's pancakes

(Continued)

(Continued)

The teacher made the following notes on discussion with the child:

- Dillon described how his marks showed all the pancakes that were made in his role play. He began to count each circle, counting accurately until he reached 28 and then he said 'lots and lots of pancakes'.
- Dillon was clearly captivated by the thought of making and eating over 100 pancakes, as described in the book.
- Dillon was eager to represent a large number, and although he was unable to write a corresponding numeral, he was confident enough to make marks, which expressed his mathematical thoughts.

Next steps:

- Provide opportunities for counting large quantities and write corresponding numerals both in focused teaching groups and when it arises naturally.
- Encourage Dillon to see numerals representing large quantities in the learning environment and ensure he has opportunities to write them.

Calculations

As children record a calculation, their graphics might include a mix of drawings, numerals, number lines and standard symbols. Often, the drawings will be pertinent to the 'maths story', related to the context in which the calculation is set. It is helpful to refer to these drawings as 'maths drawings', helping the child to differentiate between the purpose of quick, meaningful marks used to support mathematical calculation and a drawing in art. As the child becomes more confident and competent, they will gradually reduce non-standard marks and place greater emphasis on standard symbols.

Billy's PE session

Context: Mixed Reception and Y1 class (4–6 years)

As the children changed for a PE session, their teacher drew attention to all the children's shoes that were lined up in pairs after they had taken them off, and posed the question: 'I wonder how many shoes are lined up?' This caught the imagination of Billy who later decided that he would like to find out how many shoes there would be if 10 children changed for PE. He collected his resources and recorded his thinking, discovering that there would be 20 shoes (Figure 3.4).

The teacher made the following notes on discussion with the child:

- Billy described how he had drawn one pair of shoes in a ring and had done this 10 times. He then counted all of the shoes he had drawn.
- Billy is able to use these 'maths drawings' to support his thinking.
- Billy showed a clear understanding of addition as the union of sets.
- As Billy interpreted his mathematical graphics, he implied an understanding of the '+' sign although it is not written.
- Billy understands the meaning of the = sign.

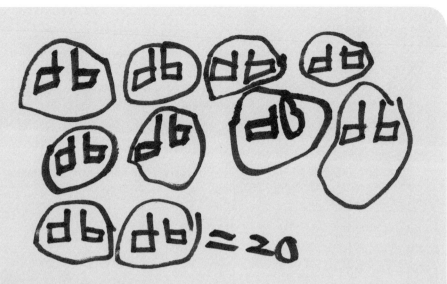

Figure 3.4   Billy's PE session

Next steps:

- Provide opportunities for Billy to see the use of standard signs modelled in a variety of situations, both in daily routines and in focused teaching sessions, reinforcing their name and meaning.
- Encourage further use in playful contexts followed by discussion to clarify any misconceptions.

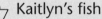 Kaitlyn's fish

Context: Mixed Reception and Y1 class (4–6 years)

Kaitlyn developed small-world play with a friend in a play tray using 10 fish and boats, where she made up a story about a fisherman catching fish. The children developed their story so that there were 15 fish and the fisherman caught 6. Kaitlyn then went on to calculate how many fish would be left, recording her graphics on a clipboard (Figure 3.5).

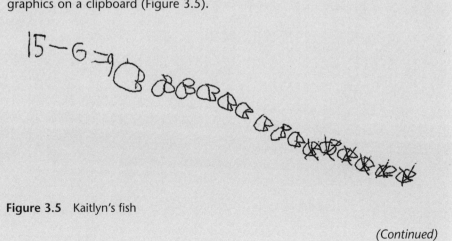

Figure 3.5   Kaitlyn's fish

(Continued)

(Continued)

The teacher made the following notes on discussion with the child:

- Kaitlyn has a sound grasp of subtraction as take away.
- Kaitlyn is confidently using standard notation here.

Next steps:

- Encourage Kaitlyn to continue to record her mathematical thinking and to share this with other children.

The bakery

Context: Year 2 (6 and 7 years)

The children had been involved in 'bakery' maths as a playful context in which to explore multiplication as repeated addition. The teacher posed a 'special offer' problem for a group of children: 'Each customer coming into the shop today gets 3 free cupcakes. Talk about and show how you could calculate how many cupcakes the bakery will need to provide.' Three children worked together on shared graphics (Figure 3.6).

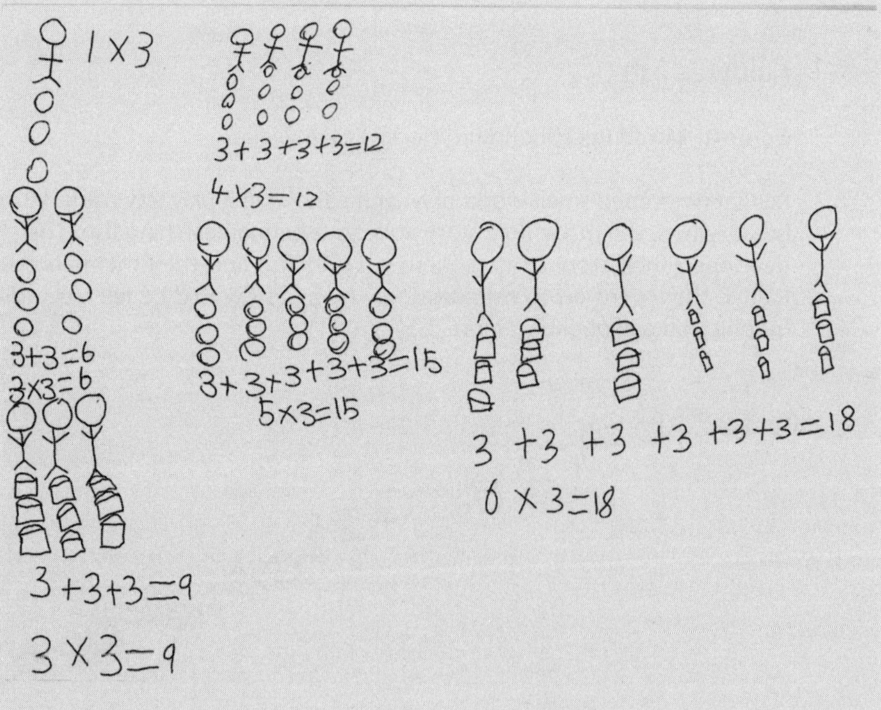

Figure 3.6 The bakery

The teacher made the following notes on discussion with the children:

- The children worked methodically, calculating the number of cakes for up to 6 customers, and their recorded work showed a mix of 'maths drawings' and standard algorithms. They were able to explain their thinking and choice of standard symbols.
- Their drawings and addition algorithms accurately reflected their thinking, although they show some misunderstanding when recording multiplication algorithms.

Next steps:

- Reinforce correct recording of multiplication algorithms and ensure children understand how, for example, $3 + 3 + 3 + 3$ is 3×4.

Principles into practice

- Avoid opening focused teaching sessions by writing an algorithm. This is likely to become copied by the children and therefore will not reflect their true thinking and understanding.
- Before the children make any mathematical marks, encourage them to talk about what they might draw or write to help them, both with the adult and with their peers.
- Model algorithms during the session when it is appropriate, after observing the children's graphics and some assessment of their understanding has been made.
- Give the children time to talk about their mathematical graphics both to one another and to the group.
- Give opportunities for children to talk about which type of graphics they found the most useful and why.

Getting started

If teachers and practitioners are currently using traditional methods for recording mathematics such as workbooks and sheets, moving wholesale to a culture of mathematical graphics will undoubtedly seem overwhelming. Ensuring that children have opportunities to create their own mathematical graphics and, most importantly, have many opportunities to see others, both adults and children, make mathematical graphics and talk about them is crucial. Table 3.1 gives some exemplars of how teachers might model written calculations in naturally occurring situations. This emergent approach, however, will only be effective in a learning culture which fully embraces its philosophy and in an environment which promotes and supports risk taking, independence, enquiry and the desire of its learners to 'be mathematicians'. This approach can be facilitated by one's day-to-day practice and continuous provision, such as the playful contexts offered in role play, play trays and small-world dramas (see Chapter 2).

One way to promote this is to introduce a time during the week in which to work with a small focused teaching group where children can 'have a go' at recording

Table 3.1 Opportunities for modelling written calculations in daily routines

Opportunity	Exemplar
Number songs	Five currant buns: Write algorithm $5 - 1 = 4$ $4 - 1 = 3$ $3 - 1 = 2$ $2 - 1 = 1$ $1 - 1 = 0$ as each bun is bought.
Discussion of lunch numbers	'There are 29 people here today. 20 people are having a school dinner. How many are having a packed lunch?' $29 - 20 = 9$
Planting seeds	There are 6 people in the group. Each person will plant 3 seeds. How many seeds will we need? $3 + 3 + 3 + 3 + 3 + 3 = 18$ $3 \times 6 = 18$
Giving out clipboards	There are 12 clipboards and 4 groups. How many clipboards will each group have? $12 \div 4 = 3$
Stacking chairs	The chairs are in 5 groups of 4. $4 + 4 + 4 + 4 + 4 = 20$ $4 \times 5 = 20$
Lining up in pairs	12 people are lining up in 2s. $2 + 2 + 2 + 2 + 2 + 2 = 12$ $2 \times 6 = 12$

their own marks; this is an unthreatening way to begin. If the children have been accustomed to recording their mathematics in more formal ways, they might find the freedom of the empty whiteboard and the invitation to 'have a go' inhibiting at first. With gentle encouragement and by ensuring that the learning environment promotes a positive culture in which children feel they can take risks, many of them will begin to find the empty whiteboard liberating.

Principles into practice

- Ensure that adults use the many opportunities that exist during the day, including interaction with independent activities, to model ways of recording mathematics and to include the use of formal symbols where appropriate and with explanation.
- Make available well-stocked collections of things with which to explore schematic play, such as baskets of shells, buttons, bricks, and so on.
- Have a well-stocked graphics area with an abundance of attractive and varied mark-making resources (see Chapter 2).
- Provide clipboards and paper beside play trays and small-world dramas to facilitate spontaneous mathematical mark making during or on reflection of play in these contexts.
- Display children's graphics and give children ownership of presenting their own marks.
- Provide a range of opportunities for children to make mathematical graphics in both focused teaching sessions and in their independent play.
- Stand back and allow children to explore their own marks, resisting the need to demand a 'right answer'.
- Avoid telling the children how to solve a problem and what marks to make.
- Give children opportunities to talk about their thinking.
- Be patient and promote a positive, enquiring and mathematics-rich environment.

Glossary

Algorithm: a step-by-step procedure for solving a specific problem, such as an addition, subtraction, multiplication or division problem.

EYFS: Early Years Foundation Stage.

Further reading

Carruthers, E. and Worthington, M. (2011) *Understanding Children's Mathematical Graphics: Beginnings in Play*. Maidenhead: Open University Press/McGraw-Hill. This book provides the theory underpinning the significance of mathematical graphics and gives numerous examples and case studies of mathematical graphics made by young children in playful contexts.

Department of Children, Schools and Families (DCSF) (2008) *Independent Review of Mathematics Teaching in Early Years Settings and Primary Schools*. London: DCSF. Here, it is useful to read first hand the importance the review places on play and mathematical graphics.

Department of Children, Schools and Families (DCSF) (2008) *Mark Making Matters: Young Children Making Meaning in all Areas of Learning and Development*. Nottingham: DCSF. This text offers practical examples of children's graphics and examples of practice.

www.childrens-mathematics.net – this website offers evidence-based research into young children's mathematical meaning making and communication, showing many examples of annotated mathematical graphics.

4

Counting and using number

This chapter covers:

- the development of counting skills, and how this can be supported
- the imaginative use of number lines and counting sticks
- early mathematical operations
- using money
- examples of focused teaching activities and examples of independent activities based on the theme of 'Handa's village'.

Counting

Learning to count proficiently involves the acquisition of skills through involvement in key experiences using the language of number and comparison (Montague-Smith and Price, 2012). Children need to:

- learn number names in order
- count objects by touching them
- understand that the last number they say is the total number of objects in the group
- transfer these skills effectively from one context to the next
- move competently from counting con-crete objects to counting abstractly.

It is crucial to provide a wide range of interesting objects, both like and unlike, for children to count and to ensure that there is a purpose for the activity, whether for the sheer joy of handling and observing tiny shells in a basket, or finding the number of play people that will fit into a vehicle made in the construction area. The practitioner must, therefore, plan carefully to ensure that the learning environment offers opportunities for counting in stimulating and meaningful ways (see Examples below).

Boxes and baskets, filled with interesting objects, can be displayed on table-tops to encourage children to observe, feel and count. The contents of these counting collections might include:

- acorns
- beads
- butter beans (that can become 'magic beans' by spray-painting them)
- buttons
- clothes pegs
- dog biscuits
- conkers

- glass pebbles/marbles
- leaves
- pasta shapes (again can be spray-painted)
- salt dough objects (theme-related)
- shells
- sunflower/pumpkin seeds.

This is most successful when these counting collections are changed frequently and are related to the current theme and interests of the youngsters. Children also need to explore the equivalence of number, and have opportunities to count in 2s, 5s and 10s (see Examples below). Counting a large number of objects in 10s, for example, allows them to explore a 'big number', and also provides children with valuable experience in preparing for place value.

There is generally an over-emphasis on the cardinal nature of number in the early years (Haylock and Cockburn, 2013). When planning artefacts for counting boxes and baskets, it is also valuable to create opportunities for children to order numbers, examples being:

- matching the number of spots on a salt dough ladybird to the corresponding numeral on leaves numbered 0–10 placed alongside

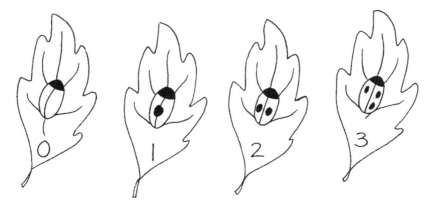

Figure 4.1   Matching number of spots to corresponding numeral

- placing the corresponding number of plastic flies on 'webs' (made of paper and string) numbered 0–10

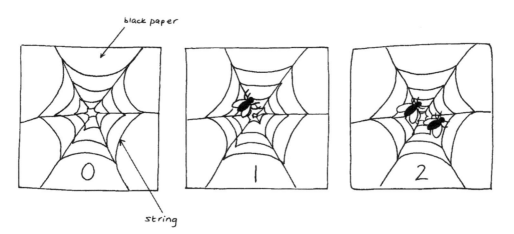

Figure 4.2   Matching number of spiders to corresponding numeral

- placing numbered model houses in numerical order.

Specific number apparatus such as Numicon® (see Resources), along with number lines and objects, allow children to explore the 'threeness of 3', for example.

Using number lines

Much is written about the value of young children's involvement with number lines in their mathematical development (Carruthers and Worthington, 2011; Haylock and Cockburn, 2013; Montague-Smith and Price, 2012). There can be an overemphasis on the cardinal aspect of number with less consideration given to encouraging young children to make connections between the cardinal and ordinal nature of number. Haylock and Cockburn (2013: 36) suggest:

> young children should do as much of their number work moving up and down number lines, or similar manifestations of the ordinal aspect, as they do manipulating sets of counters and blocks and counting objects in sets.

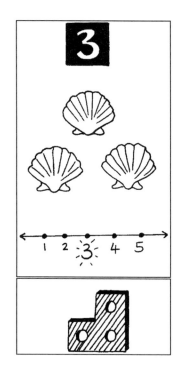

Figure 4.3   Number of interest

Young children should have access to number lines in all their forms. These include:

- number tracks
- number snakes (number tracks in the form of a snake often going up to numbers beyond 20)
- washing lines accompanied by baskets of numeral cards and pegs
- individual tracks and lines (for use with fingers or counters)
- big floor number lines and tracks (for jumping along)
- counting sticks.

Big floor number lines are particularly useful as they enable children to count the jumps they make forwards, or back along the number line, and help them experience the ordinal system in a very physical way. Some younger children find this easier than manipulating fingers or objects along smaller, individual number lines.

There are several ways of making number lines:

- numerals and line attached to a plastic carpet runner
- carpet tape stuck to indoor flooring to create a permanent number line
- number line sewn onto a long roll of hessian
- 'instant' number line using a roll of thick ribbon and numeral cards or tiles
- permanently marked number lines in the outside area.

They can be used imaginatively in practitioner-led sessions:

- featuring in maths stories as stepping stones to cross, for example
- as reference points to illustrate the connections between the ordinal and cardinal nature of number
- showing connections between the different structures of addition and subtraction (see below).

By ensuring that number lines are constantly available, both indoors and outdoors, and by allowing children time and space for their exploration, they are often incorporated into the children's own play. Such examples of their use might include:

- as numbered parking areas
- as house/shop numbers
- as rivers and stepping stones
- during children's own games with dice and other objects.

This allows children to make important connections between experience in their play and understanding of the number system.

Counting sticks

In effect, the counting stick is a form of the blank number line. Demarcated with lines at regular intervals, it is the ideal resource for counting on, or back, from any given number, counting in given units and problem solving. Commonly used throughout the primary school, it can be put to good effect in the early years in conjunction with a small puppet in a story context (see Table 8.1). By ascribing the beginning of the stick with a number, the children can count on and back in given units. It offers excellent opportunities for the use of mathematical vocabulary and problem solving. Prompts might include:

Figure 4.4 Counting stick

- I wonder, which number has the puppet landed on? How do you know?
- Can you show the same number of fingers?
- What number comes before/after?
- How many more jumps will the puppet need to get to the end?
- How many more jumps will the puppet need to go back to the beginning?
- If the puppet starts at 0, how many jumps of 2 will it need to get to 10?

As with number lines, the counting stick can be made available to children to incorporate in their own play. By providing finger puppets (frogs, caterpillars, etc.), children can retell stories from focused teaching sessions, and develop their own. Supplies of 'post-it' notes are also useful for children to write numerals on and label the counting stick as they wish.

Creative ideas for good practice

In order to promote the use of mathematical vocabulary:

- model mathematics vocabulary during daily routines and in focused teaching
- allow children time and space to use mathematical vocabulary during focused teaching sessions and encourage them to practise using these 'new' words in their independent play
- encourage the use of the 'micro-chat', where children are encouraged to talk quietly to a partner about a specific mathematical problem. This engages every child in the activity and gives them all time to speak in sentences.

Mathematical operations

The most commonly used mathematical operations in the early years are summarized in Table 4.1. Important points to consider when teaching mathematical operations are:

- Avoid over-emphasis on particular mathematical structures, typically addition as the union of two sets and subtraction as take away.
- Use number lines to highlight connections between activities and mathematical structures, such as jumping back along a number line to exemplify reduction (see Activity 4.4).

Using money

Some early years settings and schools have differing views about using real money for teaching and learning, and it is up to individual settings to establish their own guidelines about this. Undoubtedly, there are benefits in allowing children to handle, and consequently familiarize themselves with, real coins, giving the

Table 4.1 Examples of mathematical operations in playful contexts

Mathematical operation	Structure	Example of a practitioner's question in a specific learning context
Addition	• Union of two sets • Counting on	• Role play: 'Claire has 2 post bags, 1 of which has 3 letters and the other 2 letters. How many letters does Claire have altogether?' • Play tray: 'How many scoops of corn did it take to fill the sack? Samira put in 4, then 3 more'.
Subtraction	• Taking away (partitioning) • Counting back (reduction) • Difference (comparison) • Inverse of addition (complementary addition)	• Washing line: 'There are 6 sacks on the washing line. Jayesh takes 3 down. How many are left?' • Number line (on a big leaf number line 0–10): 'The ladybird is on leaf number 8. It flies 4 leaves back. Where will it land?' • Block play: 'Tilly has made her ice-cream stall with 8 wooden blocks. Sam has made his with 6. How many more wooden blocks did Tilly use?' • Role play: 'The baker must have 12 cakes on the shelf. She has already made 4, so how many more does she need to make?'
Multiplication	• Repeated addition • Scaling	• Play tray: 'I can see 4 plant pots with 2 spiders in each one. How many spiders are there altogether?' • Block play (using same-sized blocks): 'Joe's wall is 4 blocks long. Chloe wants to make a wall 2 times as long. How many blocks does she need?'
Division	• Repeated subtraction • Sharing • Grouping (inverse of multiplication)	• Role play (using a plate of 6 biscuits): 'How many times can we take 2 biscuits?' • Role play: 'We have 3 children and 9 items of washing to do. Can you share out the washing fairly?' • Malleable materials: 'How many bags of 2 bread buns do we need to make 10 bread buns?'

activities in which they are involved authenticity. Possibilities for play involving money in specific areas in the learning environment might include:

- role play – using money in 'real-life' situations
- modelling and painting – printing with coins, coin rubbings, moulds in modelling dough
- play trays – sorting coins into a selection of unusual/attractive purses or bags
- construction/technology – making simple money boxes big enough for 10 coins
- table-top counting activities – counting pennies in a 'staircase'; counting pennies in groups of 10; laying coins in a pattern.

Such experiences provide opportunities to familiarize children with the shape, colour and size of each coin in contexts that promote the use of related vocabulary (see below). Only when children are able to identify and name coins confidently are they ready to begin to make amounts. Exchange games are a useful precursor to this. The most successful of these are simply made by the practitioner or the children themselves and depict their current interests. With the use of dice, children can collect specified numbers of pennies which are then exchanged for a given coin, such as exchanging five pennies for a 5p coin.

Counting and ordering

count (up) to; count on (from, to); count back (from, to); more; less; many; few; tally; odd; even; units; ones; tens; hundreds; digit; place; place value; the same number as; as many as; equal to; greater than; more than; larger; bigger; less; fewer; smaller; greatest; most; largest; biggest; least; fewest; smallest; one more; ten more; one less; ten less; compare; order; size; ordinal names; next; between; in between; half way between; above; below

Estimating

guess how many; estimate; nearly; roughly; close to; about the same as; just over; just under; exact; exactly; too much; too little; too many; too few; enough; not enough; round; nearest; round to the nearest ten

Addition

add; more; plus; make; sum; total; altogether; score; double; near double; one more, two more, ten more, one hundred more; how many more is ... than ...?; how much more is ...?

Subtraction

subtract; take away; minus; leave; how many are left?; one less, two less, ten less, one hundred less; how many fewer is ... than ...?; how much less is ...?; how many more to make ...? (complementary addition); what is the difference between ...?

Multiplication

lots of; groups of; repeated addition; array; row; column; double

Division

share, share equally; group in pairs, threes, tens; equal groups of; divide, divided by, divided into; repeated subtraction; left, left over

Money

coin; value; amount; worth more, worth less; greater than; too expensive, less expensive; cheaper than

Examples of activities based on the stories *Handa's Surprise* and *Handa's Hen* by Eileen Browne

Activity 4.1   Baskets of mangoes

Learning objective:	Counting objects accurately and matching to the corresponding numeral.
Resources:	Numeral cards 0–10; card 'mangoes'; simple card 'baskets'; card labels; coloured pens; large floor number line.
How to begin:	Ask a group of children to prepare the mangoes to sell at market. The market will sell them in baskets of different quantities. Ask a child to take a numeral card and read it

	out. This is the number of mangoes that they will count out and put into their basket. Once the mangoes are counted out, the child writes the corresponding numeral on a label and labels the basket. Allow the children time to label several baskets.
Development:	Ask the children to swap baskets of mangoes to check that they have been counted accurately. Encourage the children to take their basket to the corresponding numeral on a large floor number line, take out the mangoes and lay them in a column above the numeral to count and check. Doing this for all the numerals along the number line helps to reinforce the connections between cardinal and ordinal numbers, and provides a clear visual image of the growing nature of the numbers 0–10.
Key vocabulary:	Number names 0–10; enough; not enough; too many; too few; more than; greater than; less than; fewer than; in a line; order; group; set.
Simplification:	Use number cards, or tiles, 0–5.
Extension:	Children are told that the mangoes are to be sold in baskets of 10s. Using random numeral cards 10–100, children work in pairs to collect a numeral card, identify the numeral on it and count out the number in groups of 10. Each group of 10 is labelled with the numeral written on it. Encourage the children to say how many groups of 10 and how many left over their numeral has. The baskets of 10, and the few remaining mangoes, provide a clear visual image of 10s and 1s.

Activity 4.2   Counting tangerines

Learning objective:	Counting in 10s.
Resources:	100 small salt dough or card tangerines; 10 small hoops; 10 labels each labelled with '10'; Numicon® plates of 10; writing materials.
How to begin:	Handa and her family have harvested many tangerines. Encourage the children to estimate how many tangerines there are and to discuss strategies to find an efficient way to count a large group of objects. If the children are unfamiliar with counting large groups of objects in 10s, suggest this as a strategy. Children count the tangerines in groups of 10, placing each 10 into a small hoop and labelling '10' with the corresponding Numicon® plate alongside, thus reinforcing quantity, numerals and Numicon® image.
Development:	Discuss how the children might make a record of what they have done, either pictorially or by using standard notation: $10 + 10 + 10 + 10 + 10 + 10 + 10 + 10 + 10 + 10 = 100$.

(Continued)

(Continued)

Key vocabulary:	Number names of tens numbers to 100; groups of 10; tens; add; makes; equals; is the same as.
Extension:	Children record as multiplication 10 x 10 = 100. Ask the children to calculate how many tangerines there would be in 7 groups of 10, 9 groups of 10, and so on.

Activity 4.3   How many pieces of fruit?

Learning objective:	Addition of two groups.
Resources:	Large floor number line 0–10; individual number lines 0–10; writing materials; per child – two card 'baskets'; 10 card passion fruits; 10 card bananas.
How to begin:	Tell the children a story about Handa and Akeyo picking fruit; Handa picks bananas and Akeyo picks passion fruit. Each day the girls pick a different number of fruits, for example Handa picks four bananas and Akeyo picks three passion fruit. How many pieces of fruit have they collected altogether?
Development:	Ask the children to calculate and record their thinking: how many fruits are collected each day? Encourage the children to see the connection between the counting on and union of two sets by 'jumping' their mark making or algorithm along the number line. Discuss their mathematical graphics and any misconceptions they might have.
Key vocabulary:	Number names 0–10; how many more; add; makes; equals; is the same as.
Simplification:	Use five pieces of fruit per child and reinforce by encouraging children to use these resources and number lines with each example. Reinforce the associated vocabulary.
Extension:	Handa and Akeyo are joined by a friend who collects a basket of guava. Children are invited to add three groups, calculate how many are collected altogether and discuss and record their thinking.

Activity 4.4   Feeding the hens

Learning objective:	Understanding the operation of subtraction and related vocabulary.
Resources:	10 'peas' (small green beads); small-world hen; big floor number line 0–10; individual number lines 0–10; writing materials.
How to begin:	Tell the children a variety of subtraction stories, giving them the opportunity to manipulate the resources with the storytelling. Stories might include: Handa has some

	peas to feed to the hens. Handa throws 10 peas to a hen and the hen eats three. How many are left? The hen ate five peas yesterday and she ate nine peas today. What is the number difference between the two amounts of peas? If the hen eats four peas in the morning, how many more has she eaten later if she eats 10 by the end of the day?
Development:	Offer the children opportunities to discuss and record mathematical graphics to illustrate each subtraction story. Ask the children to use the number line to make connections between taking away examples and the reduction structure of subtraction.
Key vocabulary:	Subtraction; take away; less than; how many are left; count back; equals; is the same as; difference; how many more to make.
Simplification:	Use five peas and reinforce by encouraging children to use materials, fingers and number lines with each example and alongside this the associated vocabulary.
Extension:	Offer a variety of different subtraction stories, such as: The large hen eats 15 peas and the small hen eats 9. What is the number difference between the amounts eaten? Ask the children to record the corresponding algorithm as both addition and subtraction and explore the relationship between the two.

Principles into practice

- Provide interesting and varied objects for children to count in meaningful situations.
- Encourage children to make links between the cardinal and ordinal nature of number.
- Use number lines frequently and make them available for children to use for reference, and to incorporate into their own play.
- Ensure children have opportunities to see and discuss the different structures of mathematical operations, avoiding over-emphasis on one.
- Model mathematical vocabulary and recording, using standard notation where appropriate.

ICT

The supermarket

Objective:	use of mathematical vocabulary for addition and subtraction.
ICT resources:	camera; laptop; projector.
Activity:	the children film supermarket role play including purchases made. The film is shown for the class/group to watch and the children identify mathematical vocabulary such as 'more than', 'less than', 'fewer', 'altogether', and discuss in the context of the 'supermarket' activity.

(Continued)

(Continued)

Daily routines

Objective:	addition as combining groups and subtraction as take away.
ICT resources:	camera; laptop; IWB.
Activity:	photos are taken of daily routines such as children eating fruit at snack time; counting fruit at snack time; children sitting with pairs of shoes after they have changed for PE. The photos in turn are then displayed on the IWB and children decide which mathematical operation the picture exemplifies. They then write the corresponding algorithm on the IWB beside the photo for discussion. This is an ideal activity to provide for children and parents as families come into school on a morning.

Find the number!

Objective:	counting objects 0–10 accurately and matching number to numeral.
ICT resource:	'talking box' (see Resources).
Activity:	a chosen number name is recorded on the 'talking box'. A child opens the box to hear the spoken number and 'helps' a puppet find the corresponding number of objects, numeral and Numicon® and places these inside the box (see Photo 4.1).

Photo 4.1 A child listens to a recorded number name on the 'talking box' and finds the corresponding Numicon® plate

Glossary

Cardinal: the number that indicates how many there are in a set.

Complementary addition: the mathematical operation that finds out how many more are needed to make a given number.

Ordinal: a number denoting the position in a sequence, such as 1st, 2nd, 3rd, etc.

Partition: the act of dividing a set of objects into two subsets.

Scaling: the process of enlargement by making a quantity a specified number of times bigger.

Further reading

Haylock, D. (2010) *Mathematics Explained for Primary Teachers*, 4th edition. London: Sage Publications. This book provides maths subject knowledge and is particularly relevant for those teaching KS2 children.

Haylock, D. and Cockburn, A. (2013) *Understanding Mathematics for Young Children*, 4th edition. London: Sage Publications. This comprehensive book provides easily accessible subject knowledge for those teaching 3–8-year-olds.

Montague-Smith, A. and Price, A.J. (2012) *Mathematics in Early Years Education*. London: Routledge. This is a clear account of how young children learn to count and use number, with practical examples.

Skinner, C. and Stevens, J. (2013) *Foundations of Mathematics: An Active Approach to Number, Shape and Measures in the Early Years*. London: Bloomsbury. This text provides practical ideas for counting and number activities.

Thompson, I. (ed.) (2008) *Teaching and Learning Early Number*, 2nd edition. Maidenhead: Open University Press/McGraw-Hill. This book contains chapters on recording and misconceptions, and is particularly relevant to primary school teachers.

www.nrich.maths.org – this website has lots of useful information about all aspects of maths, particularly number and counting, with many practical examples.

Examples of independent activities: Handa's home – a village in south-west Kenya

Example 4.1   Building a hen house

Learning context: construction area outdoors

Learning objective: estimating numbers and checking by counting

	FS	Y1	Y2
Activity	Children estimate how many large wooden bricks or crates will be needed to construct a hen house for Handa's hens. Construct and count the blocks or crates used. Test with toy/puppet hens. Develop role play.	Children estimate how many wooden bricks/Duplo® it will take to build a hen house for small-world hens. Record the estimate. Construct the hen house, test with and count the number of bricks used. Record the number used. Develop related role play.	As Y1, but using Lego®.
Resources	Large wooden blocks or crates; puppet or soft toy hens; writing materials.	Small wooden bricks/Duplo®; small-world hens; clipboard and writing materials.	Lego®; small-world hens; clipboard and writing materials.
Prompt and key questions	How can you build a hen house for Handa's hens? How many wooden blocks do you think you will need? How many did you use? Was your guess right? Which number was the biggest: your guess or the number you used? Was the number you guessed and the number you used the same?	Can you estimate how many wooden bricks/pieces of Duplo® you will need? Can you record your estimate and the actual number of bricks used? Which is greatest, or do your recordings show equal numbers?	Estimate and record how many pieces of Lego® you will need. Which is greatest: your estimate or the actual number of bricks used, or are they equal numbers? What is the difference between your estimate and the actual number of bricks?
Key vocabulary	• guess (estimate) • vocabulary of number • more than/greater than • less than/smaller than • the same	• estimate • accurate • more than/less than • equal numbers	• estimate • actual • accurate • equal numbers
Opportunities for assessment	• uses vocabulary of number • can make a sensible guess (estimate) • shows an understanding of more than/less than • can recognize when two numbers are equal	• makes a sensible estimate • can count objects accurately • can recognize when two numbers are equal	• makes a sensible estimate • can talk about difference

Links with Y3: Activity

Children estimate and record how many Lego® bricks it will take to build a hen house that has walls of 10cm long and a height of 6cm. Round this number to the nearest 10. Build the hen house and count the number of bricks used. Round to nearest 10. How close was the estimate to the actual? Calculate and record.

ELG and PNS linked objectives

• FS: Count reliably with numbers from 1 to 20 (ELG)
• Y1: Estimate a number that can be checked by counting (PNS)
• Y2: Estimate a number of objects (PNS)
• Y3: Round two-digit or three-digit numbers to nearest 10 or 100 and give estimates for their sums and differences (PNS)

Example 4.2   River animals

Learning context: play tray

Learning objective: counting large groups of objects reliably and beginning to count in steps of 2s, 5s and 10s

	FS	Y1	Y2
Activity	Children count out two animals and place them on different areas of the river, such as the rocks, log, boat, waterfall, trees on the bank. Develop small-world play.	Children group animals in numbers of their choice around different areas of the river and record what they have done. Develop small-world play.	Children put animals into groups and develop small-world play. The animals like to be in pairs. Explore whether the groups of animals are odd or even by putting them in pairs. Record findings on a clipboard. Develop small-world play.
Resources	Large selection (more than 20) of African wild animals such as hippo, geese, crocodiles, large birds, elephants; green river water (using green food colouring); pebbles; small-world boats; driftwood.	As FS, plus clipboard and writing materials.	As Y1.
Prompt and key questions	The animals like to explore the river with a partner. Give each animal a partner and find a place in the river they would like to explore. How many animals are there? Try counting in 2s.	The animals like to explore different parts of the river in groups. Decide how many animals you would like to have in each group. Can you record how many you have in each group? What do you know about that number?	Do the animals in your groups each have a partner? What do you know about each of those numbers? Explain and make a record of your thinking.
Key vocabulary	• vocabulary of number • count on • more than/greater than • pair	• vocabulary of number • more than/greater than • greatest/smallest	• odd • even
Opportunities for assessment	• counts out 2 accurately • uses vocabulary of numbers • successfully counts in 2s	• counts objects accurately • can record numerals • can order numbers recorded	• shows an understanding of odd and even numbers • can record and discuss reasoning

Links with Y3: Activity

Map the wildlife living in the area. Draw a picture map of the river with groups of animals at various points. Count the animals you have recorded in groups of 2s, 5s and 10s. Which grouping was the most appropriate? Why?

ELG and PNS linked objectives

- FS: Count reliably with numbers from 1 to 20 (ELG) and count in 2s (PNS)
- Y1: Count reliably at least 20 objects, recognizing that when rearranged the number of objects stays the same (PNS)
- Y2: Recognize odd and even numbers (PNS)
- Y3: Count on from and back to zero in single-digit steps or multiples of 10 (PNS)

Example 4.3   To market

Learning context: small-world play

Learning objective: calculating doubles and halves

	FS	Y1	Y2
Activity	Children count out equal numbers of animals for Handa and Akeyo to take to market. Children count the total number of animals that are being taken to market. Develop small-world play.	Children take a 'market card' telling them how many animals Handa and Akeyo will take to market. Children count out the corresponding number of animals for Handa and Akeyo, and count how many animals will be going to market altogether. Record the number each character has taken and its double. Develop small-world play.	Children take a 'market card' and halve the number shown. They count out this number of animals and give the corresponding number of animals to Handa and Akeyo. Record the operation using appropriate symbols. Develop small-world play.
Resources	Green cloth; sticks; pebbles; small blocks and pine cones (for enclosure making); two play people; small-world animals (goats, sheep, hens).	In addition to FS: pack of 'market cards' (numeral cards 1–5); clipboard and writing materials.	In addition to FS: pack of 'market cards' (numeral cards of even numbers from 2 to 20); clipboard and writing materials.
Prompt and key questions	Handa and Akeyo take a group of animals to market. They take exactly the same number of animals. Choose how many they will take. How many animals are going to market altogether? If each girl takes 4 animals, how many animals will be going to market?	Handa's aunt leaves the market cards telling the girls how many animals they can take to market on each journey. Take a card and calculate its double. Repeat for different journeys. What do you notice? Can you find a way of recording what the girls have done to show Handa's aunt?	Handa's aunt leaves the market cards telling the girls how many animals they can take to market on each journey. Take a market card. Each girl will take half this number of animals to market. Can you find a way of recording what the girls have done to show Handa's aunt?
Key vocabulary	• counting on • more than • altogether	• more than • double • half • addition	• half • double • less than • division
Opportunities for assessment	• can count out specified number accurately • uses vocabulary of counting • uses counting on to check total	• understands the concept of 'double' • can calculate double by manipulating objects or has quick mental recall • uses + and = signs accurately to record response	• shows understanding of halving • can calculate half by manipulating objects or has quick mental recall • uses ÷ sign accurately to record response

Links with Y3: Activity

Using 'market cards' showing even numbers from 20 to 100, calculate half the number shown on the card. How can you check your answer?

ELG and PNS linked objectives

• FS: Solve problems including doubling and halving (ELG)
• Y1: Recall doubles of all numbers to at least 10 (PNS)
• Y2: Understand that halving is the inverse of doubling (PNS)
• Y3: Use knowledge of number operations and corresponding inverses, including doubling and halving, to estimate and check calculations (PNS)

Example 4.4   Fruit for lunch

Learning context: malleable materials

Learning objective: counting and grouping objects in 2s, 5s and 10s

	FS	Y1	Y2
Activity	Children make a variety of fruits with modelling dough, making two pieces of each fruit. Count fruit in 2s.	Children make a variety of fruits with modelling dough and count them in 10s.	Children make as many different fruits with modelling dough as they can in 3 minutes. Count the fruit by grouping in 2s, 5s or 10s and find out who has made the most.
Resources	Coloured modelling dough.	Coloured modelling dough; paper plates; writing materials.	Coloured modelling dough; 3-minute timer.
Prompt and key questions	Handa and Akeyo want to eat the same fruit for lunch. Use the modelling dough to make different fruits, making sure that there are two pieces of each fruit. How many pieces of fruit have you made altogether? Count them in 2s.	Handa is expecting many family and friends to join her for lunch. Use the modelling dough to make lots of different fruit and put 10 pieces of fruit on each plate. Counting in 10s, find out how many pieces of fruit you have made and record this number. More and more people arrive at Handa's home. Calculate and record how many pieces of fruit you will have if you had 10 more.	You have 3 minutes to prepare as many different fruits as you can. How many do you think you will make? Choose a way to group the fruit you have made and count them in 2s, 5s or 10s. Which way of counting worked best? Why?
Key vocabulary	• number names • even numbers	• number names • groups of 10	• estimate • actual • multiples of 2, 5, 10
Opportunities for assessment	• uses vocabulary of counting • recognizes even numbers • counts aloud in 2s • counts group of objects accurately in 2s	• uses vocabulary of counting • counts groups of objects accurately in 10s • can say the number that is 10 more than a given number	• can make a sensible estimate • can count a group of objects in a chosen way accurately • shows understanding of multiples

Links with Y3: Activity

As Y2. In addition, record the counting steps taken. What pattern do you notice?

ELG and PNS linked objectives

- FS: Count aloud in 2s (PNS)
- Y1: Say the number that is 10 more or less for multiples of 10 (PNS)
- Y2: Count up to 100 objects by grouping them in 2s, 5s or 10s (PNS)
- Y3: Count on from or back to zero in single-digit steps or multiples of 10 (PNS)

Example 4.5   Fruit selection

Learning context: washing line

Learning objective: beginning to use knowledge of place value to order numbers

	FS	Y1	Y2
Activity	Children select and peg 21 card fruits, each marked with a numeral 0–20, along a washing line.	As FS.	Children peg 20 card fruits marked with random numbers 0–100 along a washing line.
Resources	Laminated card fruits, each marked with a numeral 0–20; clothes pegs; washing line.	As FS.	As FS, but with 20 card fruits marked with random numerals between 0 and 100.
Prompt and key questions	Handa has picked a lot of fruit and is placing them in the order in which she picked them. Put the fruits in order along the washing line. Which fruit did she pick before the banana? Which fruit did she pick after the banana? Which fruits did she pick in between the guava and the tangerine?	In addition to FS: What do you know about the digit 1 in 15?	Some animals have eaten some of the collected fruit. Put the remaining fruit in order on the washing line. Which numbers are the greatest/smallest?
Key vocabulary	• number names • order • more than/greater than • smaller than/less than • in between	• numerical order • more than/greater than • less than/smaller than • in between	• numerical order • more than/greater than • less than/smaller than • in between
Opportunities for assessment	• recognizes and names numerals 0–20 • uses vocabulary of number • uses vocabulary of more than/less than • orders numerals 0–20 accurately	• recognizes and names numerals 0–20 • orders numerals 0–20 accurately • identifies numbers in between two given numbers	• recognizes and names given numerals 0–100 • displays understanding of place value

Links with Y3: Activity

Make individual number lines on which to order 20 pictures of fruit randomly numbered from 0 to 100.

ELG and PNS linked objectives

- FS: Count reliably with numbers from one to 20, place them in order and say which is one more or one less than a given number (ELG)
- Y1: Use knowledge of place value to position numbers 0–20 on a number track and number line (PNS)
- Y2: Order two-digit numbers and position them on a number line (PNS)
- Y3: Read, write and order whole numbers of at least 100 and position them on a number line (PNS)

Example 4.6   Cows and goats

Learning context: small world

Learning objective: deriving and recalling pairs of numbers with a total of 10 (and 20)

	FS	Y1	Y2
Activity	Children use materials to construct two enclosures. Place a chosen number of animals in one enclosure and the remaining animals in the other. Draw a representation for Akeyo. Develop small-world play.	Children use materials to construct two enclosures and find as many ways as they can of housing 10 animals between them. Record their findings. Develop small-world play.	As for Y1, but using 20 animals.
Resources	Small-world play animals (cows and goats); twigs; pebbles; bark; etc. (for enclosure making); play people; clipboard and writing materials.	As FS.	As FS, but using 20 animals.
Prompt and key questions	Akeyo needs to house 10 goats and cows in two enclosures. Build two enclosures and explore the different arrangements of animals she could have. How can the 10 animals be housed? How many different ways can you find? Can you find a way of making a record for Akeyo showing the ways you have found?	Akeyo needs to house 10 animals in two enclosures. Build two enclosures and find, and record, as many ways as you can of housing the animals. Are all the ways you have found different? How many ways did you find? What do you notice about your records?	Akeyo needs to house 20 animals in two enclosures. Find, and record, all the ways the animals can be housed. How many different ways are there? What do you notice about your results?
Key vocabulary	• vocabulary of number • add • more than/greater than • altogether	• addition • more than/greater than • pairs of numbers	• more than/greater than • addition facts
Opportunities for assessment	• uses vocabulary of number • can count the total number of objects • can record pictorially/ uses + and = symbols with understanding	• can calculate by manipulating objects/ quick recall of known number facts • can record using + and = symbols accurately and with understanding	• can calculate by manipulating objects/ quick recall of known number facts • can record using + and = symbols accurately and with understanding

Links with Y3: Activity

Using numeral cards 0–100, take one card. This is the number of animals to be placed in one enclosure. Now calculate the number of animals needed in the other enclosure to make 100. How can you record this? How can you check?

ELG and PNS linked objectives

- FS: Using quantities and objects, add single two-digit numbers (ELG). Select two groups of objects to make a given total of objects (PNS)
- Y1: Derive and recall all pairs of numbers with a total of 10 (PNS)
- Y2: Derive and recall all addition facts for each number to at least 10 and all pairs with totals of 20 (PNS)
- Y3: Derive and recall all addition and subtraction facts for each number to 20, sums and differences of multiples of 10 and number pairs that total 100 (PNS)

Example 4.7 Mathematical fishing

Learning context: play tray

Learning objective: solving problems involving all four mathematical operations

	FS	Y1	Y2
Activity	Children catch laminated card fish, labelled with numerals 0–10, with a fishing rod. Identify the numeral and compare with other numerals caught.	Children catch two laminated card fish, labelled with numerals 0–10, with a fishing rod. Children add the two numbers together and record their calculation.	Children catch two laminated card fish, labelled with numerals 0–10, with a fishing rod. Choose a calculation they can make using the two numbers. Discuss and check with a partner and record as +, −, x or ÷.
Resources	Green/blue fabric to line play tray; laminated card fish each with a numeral 0–10 and a paper clip; fishing rods (doweling, string and small magnet secured to the end).	As for FS but use numerals 0–20; clipboard and writing materials.	As Y1.
Prompt and key questions	Handa's family fish for tiger fish. Can you catch 'mathematical fish' with a friend? What do you know about the number you caught? Is your number greater or smaller than the number caught by your friend?	Catch two mathematical fish and add the numbers together. Record your calculation. Compare your calculations with those of your friend. What do you notice? Are any of your calculations the same?	Catch two mathematical fish and decide on a calculation you can do using the numbers you have caught. Which mathematical operation will you use? Record your calculations and compare with those of a friend. Are they the same or different?
Key vocabulary	• number names • more than/less than	• number names • addition • add • plus • altogether • more than/less than	• addition/add/plus/and more • subtraction/take away/minus • multiply/times/repeated addition • division/divide/group/share • equals/makes/is the same as
Opportunities for assessment	• uses vocabulary of number accurately • recognizes and names numerals 0–10 • uses vocabulary of more than/less than	• recognizes and names numerals 0–20 • calculates accurately using chosen method • has recall of known facts • can record using = and + signs accurately and with understanding	• recognizes and names numerals 0–20 • calculates accurately using chosen method • can record using +, −, ÷, x, = accurately and with understanding

Links with Y3: Activity

Catch two fish. Choose a multiplication or division calculation you can do with these numbers. Make a record of your catches and calculations.

ELG and PNS linked objectives

- FS: Recognize numerals 1–9 (PNS)
- Y1: Recognize that addition can be done in any order (PNS)
- Y2: Use the symbols of +, −, x, ÷ and = to record and interpret number sentences involving all four operations (PNS)
- Y3: Use practical and informal written methods to multiply and divide two-digit numbers (PNS)

Example 4.8   Shopping in the supermarket

Learning context: role play

Learning objective: solving problems involving money

	FS	Y1	Y2
Activity	Children select and buy goods. Develop role play.	Children select and buy goods up to the value of £1, giving change where necessary. Develop role play.	Children calculate 'takings' in the till and enter the sum in the 'accounts book' using £.p notation. Develop role play.
Resources	Shop till; coins 1p to £2; credit card; priced goods up to £1; telephone; calendar; 'order book'; writing materials; purses; bags; paper bags; bucket balance; dressing-up clothes.	As FS.	In addition to FS: 'accounts book'.
Prompt and key questions	The supermarket is selling goods imported from Kenya such as coffee, fruit and cotton clothes. Which goods would you like to buy? How much do they cost and which coins will you use to make that value? Which coins do you have the most/fewest of?	As FS. In addition: Do you need any change? How much change will you need? How did you calculate that?	As Y1. In addition: Can you keep a record of what was sold and how much money is taken? Record this in the accounts book using £.p notation.
Key vocabulary	• value names of coins • value • amount	• value names of coins • value • amount • purchase • more expensive • cheaper than • change	• total amount • sum of • pounds and pence
Opportunities for assessment	• can sort for like coins • uses vocabulary of money • uses vocabulary of counting	• recognizes and names all coins to £1 • can make values to £1 • can calculate change from £1	• calculates total amount accurately • correctly uses £.p notation

Links with KS2: Activity

Choose three things in the shop you would like to buy. How much will you have to spend to buy them all? You only have a £5 note. How much change will you get? Record your calculation. How can you check it?

ELG and PNS linked objectives

• FS: Use everyday language to talk about money to compare quantities (prices) and to solve problems (ELG)
• Y1: Solve problems involving money, for example to 'pay' and 'give change' (PNS)
• Y2: Solve problems involving addition in contexts of pounds and pence (PNS)
• Y3: Solve one-step and two-step problems involving money, choosing and carrying out appropriate calculations (PNS)

5

Pattern

This chapter covers:

- pattern as a precursor to algebra
- understanding pattern
- patterns in the environment
- examples of focused teaching activities and recorded work, along with independent activities based on the theme of 'clothes'.

Pattern has often been under-represented in the early years mathematics curriculum and has not enjoyed the high profile that counting and using number have (Pound, 2008). Sadly, all too often, young children's experience of 'pattern work' consists of activities with pegs, beads and colouring in. Pattern, of course, exists way beyond the peg board and bead tray, and in its various forms can be seen, experienced and heard throughout daily life. In mathematics, pattern is concerned with the relationships between shapes and numbers and it is because of this that pattern is the precursor to algebra. Consequently, it is a fundamental aspect of early years mathematics. It is because of these relationships and connections that it can never be taught successfully as a 'stand-alone' unit of work. To do so would be to deprive young children of the opportunity to make their own discoveries about pattern and to make meaningful connections between pattern and their everyday experiences.

Understanding pattern

Pattern is the arrangement of shapes, numbers and actions that follow given criteria. We can:

- see pattern (in shapes or numbers)
- hear pattern (in repeated sequences of music)
- feel pattern (clapping a pattern or rhythm, or moving in a repeated sequence).

In order to be aware of and excited by pattern, young children should have the opportunity to discover, explore and create patterns in a variety of ways. Central to developing an understanding about pattern is children's ability to identify, sort for and discuss similarities and differences. They will also need to understand order and have at their disposal language such as: first, next, after, before, in between, last. It is helpful to encourage children to clap a pattern that they have observed. For example, an ABAB pattern can be clapped as: 'hands, knees, hands, knees', or an ABBA pattern as: 'hands, knees, knees, hands'. This is beneficial in that it helps the children 'feel' the pattern, enabling them to understand how the similarities and differences they observe in one situation can be transferred to another. Indeed, Haylock and Cockburn (2013) suggest that when we consider number patterns what we are in fact doing is making a connection between the relationship between the numbers and a visual image. This is clearly seen when exploring odd and even numbers while counting out objects:

- When pairing the objects, the odd numbers are 'without a partner', while the even numbers all 'have a partner'.
- Numicon® plates representing an odd number have a piece 'sticking up', while the even number plates have a 'flat top'.

☀ Creative ideas for good practice

As part of a theme where children are folding clothes and blankets, or using tablecloths in their activities, unfold a square tablecloth or sheet to reveal the square, oblong, square, oblong shapes that emerge in a pattern with each unfolding. Encourage talk about the pattern. By clapping the hands, knees, hands, knees and saying the pattern 'square, oblong, square, oblong', the children can make meaningful connections between the seeing, doing and saying of their pattern observation.

Patterns appear in different forms and can be grouped together as follows:

Repeated patterns
Children copy and create sequences, such as:

- laying a toy ladybird, bee and spider in a line as they travel into a plant pot in a small-world drama, giving opportunities to talk about which minibeast is first, which is next and which is last, along with first, second and third. This sequence can then be repeated, and it is this understanding of doing the sequence over and over again that informs the child's understanding of pattern going on and on

- clapping a sequence of sounds, such as slow, quick, quick, and repeating this over and over again.

Increasing patterns

- Constructing number 'staircases', by placing the number of objects in a column above the corresponding numeral on a number line, illustrates the connections between the ordinal and cardinal aspects of number, and therefore the pattern in the number system itself.
- Using objects in conjunction with a number line in this way allows children to see clear images, for example of odd or even numbers where alternate columns of objects increase by two each time, and for doubles along a number line beyond 10.
- Allowing young children the time and space to explore a large hundred square, either presented on a board they can handle or on the floor, provides fantastic opportunities for them to spot patterns of numbers in columns, rows and diagonally. As with number lines, hundred squares made available in the graphics area and presented on large boards in the inside and outside environments encourage children to incorporate them into their own play.
- Increasing patterns can also be explored by constructing walls, stairs and platforms with construction kits, and columns of blocks, or pictograms in data-handling work.

Line patterns

- Objects from the natural world such as leaves and shells.
- Fabric designs.
- Works of art (see 'Pattern in art' below).

Children can be encouraged to observe these patterns and reproduce them using a variety of media: paint, clay, modelling dough or fabric and thread. Working with line patterns provides excellent opportunities to explore vocabulary such as: wavy, curved, zigzag, straight, bendy, arched, spiky, thick and thin, among others. This vocabulary can then act as 'movement' vocabulary, providing a basis for work in dance where the children use the words to stimulate a series of moves which are then repeated to create a sequence of movement. Percussion instruments can be used to accompany this, thus bringing together seeing pattern, moving pattern and hearing pattern.

Identifying pattern in the world around us

Pattern in art

Works of art are a fantastic stimulus for the exploration of pattern (see Resources). They provide a visual stimulus for children to copy or to inspire their own pattern making using a variety of media. Particularly useful works include:

Andy Goldsworthy

Photographs of his sculptures using natural materials act as great inspiration for children to construct their own sculptures in repeating patterns. They can be done on a large scale during a visit to the beach using shells, driftwood, seaweed and other natural materials, or in a large, flat play tray in the outside play area.

They can also be achieved on a small scale using natural materials on pieces of black card.

Paul Klee
Much of Klee's work consists of pictures made with blocks of colour. This can inspire pictures made of colour patterns in paint, or applique work with fabric and thread.

William Morris
The repeating patterns featured in Morris's fabric and tiles provide ideas for young children and illustrate well how repeating patterns can work together to create a large piece of fabric, or cover a wall in tiles.

Bridget Riley
Her easily accessible paintings depict clear blocks of colour, often in repeating patterns.

Traditional African, Indian and Islamic art
These works of art often depict clear repeating patterns and line patterns. Indian pieces particularly often have clear repeating patterns around their borders.

Pattern in the learning environment

Practitioners can organize their learning environments to raise the profile of pattern through their displays, organization of resources and daily activities. By modelling pattern making, in the way resources are presented for example, practitioners can heighten the awareness of young children to pattern. Youngsters very soon realize that pattern is all around them and woven into their daily lives. By planning for and modelling pattern, practitioners are more likely to encourage children to become engaged in 'pattern spotting' and to be excited by it.

Creative ideas for good practice

- Set out equipment such as vehicles in the outside play area, in a repeated pattern such as lorry, bike, lorry, bike, and so on.
- Provide interactive displays that can be changed regularly, such as:

    o big/small paper flowers
    o painted bees/butterflies
    o wide/narrow paper leaves
    o paper leaves/flowers.

All of these can be presented along a paper 'vine' which extends around the classroom. Other interactive displays might include:

    o a washing line on which to hang 'washing' in a different repeated pattern each day
    o flags (bunting) displayed in a colour or shape pattern.

- Introduce pattern into daily routines, such as giving things out in a pattern, asking children to line up in a pattern, looking for patterns in lunch or snack preferences.

Pattern in the natural world

The natural world also provides a rich source of pattern. Encouraging children to collect, observe and, where appropriate, print with a selection of leaves, shells and stones enables them to see that pattern is not always manufactured. It is also important to draw children's attention to the natural patterns of day and night and the cyclical pattern of the seasons. Animal life cycles are also important to consider.

Pattern in music and song

Listening to music and music making provide many opportunities to identify and copy patterns. Children can:

- respond in movement to repeated rhythms they hear, and in a variety of media
- clap the rhythm of their name as they repeat their name over and over again and clap the syllables they hear
- use percussion instruments to create short, repeated rhythms and develop their own notation to record the quality of the patterns created.

There is a wealth of well-known and traditional songs which involve pattern, such as counting on and back in 2s or 1s ('Five currant buns') and increasing patterns ('One man went to mow'). There are many good mathematical song books available which include notes about the areas of mathematics they represent (see Resources). By making reference to a large number line during singing number songs, the practitioner can highlight the significance of pattern in each song, and help the children make valuable connections between the meaningful images the songs create for them, and patterns in the number system.

---

continue; sequence; every other one; the same, different; rule; repeating pattern; on-and-on; predict

---

Examples of activities

Activity 5.1   The sock store

Learning objective:	Counting in 2s and odd and even numbers.
Resources:	Washing line; 5 pairs of plain socks; 5 pairs of patterned socks; clothes pegs; Numicon®; individual number lines (1 per child); 5 pegs per child.
How to begin:	The shop assistant in the sock store likes to display the socks in a repeating pattern. Peg socks on to the washing line (one peg per sock) in a repeating pattern such as plain, plain, patterned, patterned, etc. Ask the children to discuss and identify the repeating pattern and encourage them to clap the observed pattern. Explain that the assistant needs to find out how many pegs she will need to peg out 5 pairs of socks. Ask the children how many pegs have been used so far and encourage them to count in twos.

Development:	Ask the children to put a peg by each even number on their number line as they count 0, 2, 4, 6, and so on. Encourage them to discuss what they notice about the position on the number line and draw their attention to the odd, even, odd, even pattern that emerges.
Key vocabulary:	Number names; how many; odd; even; pairs; before; after; next; in between.
Simplification:	Encourage the children to construct a simple, repeating pattern, naming the criteria and clapping the pattern.
Extension:	Ask the children to continue the pattern beyond 10 and to predict what would emerge.

Activity 5.2   Making wrapping paper

Learning objective:	Making and describing patterns.
Resources:	A selection of fabric from a variety of cultures depicting line and repeating patterns; squares of press print (or polystyrene); printing rollers; paper; paint; pencils.
How to begin:	Ask the children to look at the fabric and to describe the shapes, colours and patterns they see. Ask them to identify and describe these repeating patterns and talk about their preferences with a friend. Invite them to design and make a printing block that can be used to make wrapping paper, showing repeating patterns for the clothes shop.
Development:	Ask the children to score a design on their press print using ideas from the fabric they have seen. Using paint, the children fill their paper with repeating patterns and describe their work, commenting on the shapes, colours and repeats they have used.
Key vocabulary:	Swirl; curved; wavy, straight; zigzag; before; next; repeated.
Simplification:	Use simple tools to print with, such as shells, corks, pine cones, string, etc.
Extension:	Make two printing blocks and, using different colours, make different patterns on each row, describing the type of pattern they are, such as AABB, ABAB, ABBABB, etc.

Activity 5.3   Buying clothes at the clothes shop

Learning objective:	Seeing patterns in number calculations.
Resources:	10 sets of 10 items of clothing (either real or paper silhouettes); whiteboards and pens (1 per child); big floor number line 0–10; individual number lines 0–10.
How to begin:	Ask the children to keep a record for the shopkeeper of all the clothes sold. There are 10 items of clothing for sale on each 'shelf'. Ask a child to come and 'buy' 1 item of clothing from one of the piles and tell the group how many items are left in that pile. Ask the children to record the corresponding algorithm, or graphics, on their

(Continued)

(Continued)

	whiteboard. Invite a child to represent the algorithm 10 − 1 = 9 on the big floor number line by starting at 10 and jumping back 1. Other children can be involved by using their fingers to jump back on their individual number lines. This helps to make the connection between the take away and reduction structures of subtraction.
Development:	Ask another child to 'buy' two items from the next pile, three items from the next and so on, asking the children to record the corresponding algorithm for each purchase. Encourage the children to discuss any patterns they notice (10 − 1 = 9, 10 − 2 = 8, 10 − 3 = 7, 10 − 4 = 6, etc.) and ask them if they can continue the patterns in their recording until all the clothes are 'sold'.
Key vocabulary:	Less than; more than; increase; decrease; subtract; equals; is the same as.
Extension:	Ask the children to predict and record the pattern of sales that would emerge if two items of clothing were bought each time.

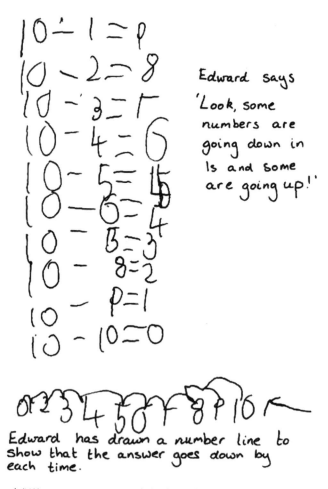

Figure 5.1   Edward (Y1) can use patterns of similar calculations

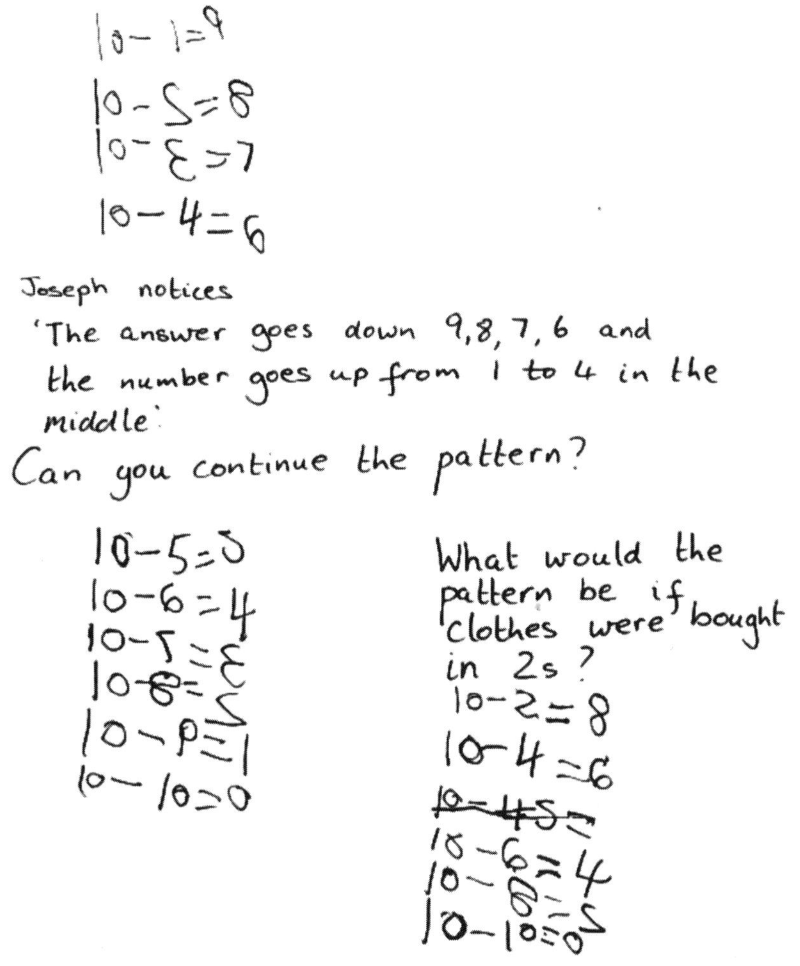

$$10 - 1 = 9$$
$$10 - 5 = 8$$
$$10 - 3 = 7$$
$$10 - 4 = 6$$

Joseph notices
'The answer goes down 9, 8, 7, 6 and the number goes up from 1 to 4 in the middle.'

Can you continue the pattern?

$$10 - 5 = 5$$
$$10 - 6 = 4$$
$$10 - 7 = 3$$
$$10 - 8 = 2$$
$$10 - 9 = 1$$
$$10 - 10 = 0$$

What would the pattern be if clothes were bought in 2s?

$$10 - 2 = 8$$
$$10 - 4 = 6$$
$$10 - 5 =$$
$$10 - 6 = 4$$
$$10 - 8 =$$
$$10 - 10 = 0$$

Figure 5.2   Joseph (Y2) uses patterns of similar calculations

Activity 5.4   Designing clothes

Learning objective:	Making and describing patterns and pictures.
Resources:	A selection of percussion instruments; large paper cut-outs of items of clothing; drawing materials.
How to begin:	Encourage the children to explore the instruments and make simple repeated rhythms.
Development:	Ask the children to represent this sound pattern by drawing, using this pattern to decorate the cut-out clothing shapes. Encourage them to talk to a partner about their patterns and how they can change them to make rows of differing patterns.
Key vocabulary:	Curvy; straight; zigzag; swirly; sharp; thick; thin.
Simplification:	Children copy a simple repeated rhythm made by the practitioner. The practitioner models how this can be transferred into graphics on a paper cut-out, and children continue the pattern.

ICT

Button patterns

Objective:	continue and copy a simple repeating pattern.
ICT resource:	SMART interactive table.
Activity:	children use small coloured 2D shapes as 'buttons' on the table to copy and create repeating patterns for the clothes factory.

Leaf fabric

Objective:	continue and copy a simple repeating pattern.
ICT resources:	visualizer; laptop; IWB; printer.
Activity:	children observe patterns in natural materials such as a selection of leaves. Children then recreate some of the repeating patterns observed using virtual pens on the IWB. These 'designs' can then be printed for the clothes factory.

Fabric textures

Objective:	continue and copy a simple repeating pattern.
ICT resources:	digital-microscope (see Resources); laptop; projector.
Activity:	children use the microscope to investigate the appearance of a range of different fabrics and discuss the differences in texture of the fabrics. Children select 2 or 3 favourite fabrics and, using photos of the fabric, create a repeating pattern 'sample' of mixed fabric for the factory.

Glossary

Sequence: objects, shapes or numbers arranged in a line, such as cow, sheep, cow, pig. When this is repeated several times, it forms a repeating pattern.

Creative ideas for good practice

- Model pattern making in the learning environment through the setting out of resources, use of displays and daily activities.
- Avoid teaching pattern as a 'unit of work', but instead highlight it in all daily activities and mathematical events as it occurs.
- Provide opportunities for children to see, hear and feel pattern through works of art, music and dance.
- Encourage children to both observe and create patterns in a variety of media.
- Encourage children to talk about the patterns they see and create, and to identify the types of pattern they are (whether ABAB, AABB, etc.).

Further reading

Montague-Smith, A. and Price, A.J. (2012) *Mathematics in Early Years Education*. London: Routledge. This text contains a comprehensive chapter on how children develop an understanding of pattern, with many practical examples.

Pound, L. (2008) *Thinking and Learning about Mathematics in the Early Years*. London: Routledge. This book has a chapter about the importance of identifying pattern in the early years, with some practical examples.

Thompson, I. (ed.) (2008) *Teaching and Learning Early Number*, 2nd edition. Maidenhead: Open University Press/McGraw-Hill. This book contains a chapter on preparation for algebra and is therefore relevant for primary school teachers.

Examples of independent activities: Clothes

Example 5.1   Clothes shop

Learning context: construction area

Learning objectives: exploring patterns involving shapes

	FS	Y1	Y2
Activity	Children use construction materials to build a 'clothes shop', laying construction materials in a pattern as they do so. Develop builders' role play.	As FS, but children also record a 'plan' of the building they construct.	As FS, but children begin by drawing a design of the building and pattern they are going to construct.
Resources	Large wooden blocks of varying sizes; plastic crates; clipboards; writing materials; builders' role-play resources.	A wide selection of small 3D solid shapes; clipboards and writing materials.	As Y1.
Prompt and key questions	Can you use the blocks to build a clothes shop? The owner wants the design of the shop front to show a pattern. How can you arrange the different blocks to show a pattern? What comes next/before/in between? Can you describe the pattern you have made? Can you draw your building?	Can you use the wooden blocks to build a clothes shop? The owner wants the design of the shop front to show a pattern. How can you construct your building? What shapes have you used? What sort of pattern is it? Can you draw your building and describe the pattern you have made for the owner?	The owner of a clothes shop wants you to draw a design for a new building using bricks in a pattern. Can you draw a design, then build the clothes shop? What bricks have you used? What sort of pattern is it? Why did you choose this pattern? Are there enough bricks to continue the pattern if you built another shop?
Key vocabulary	• position • arrange • the same • different • before • after • in between • pattern • standing up • lying down • shape names	• position • arrange • repeating pattern • the same • different • cube • cuboid • cone • arch	• position • arrangement • repeating pattern • cube • cuboid • sphere • cone • square-based pyramid
Opportunities for assessment	• selects blocks to create a sequence and copies this to make a pattern • can describe the pattern made using appropriate mathematical language	• selects and names shapes to construct pattern • can describe the type of pattern made (ABAB etc.) • can reproduce the pattern accurately in a drawing	• can draw the design showing the repeating pattern • can follow the design to construct the pattern with bricks • uses mathematical language to talk about the pattern and identify its type

Links with Y3: Activity

Boxes of clothes arrive for the new shop. On Monday 5 arrive, on Tuesday 10, on Wednesday 15 and on Thursday 20. What do you notice? How many will arrive on Friday? There are now deliveries on a Saturday or Sunday, so how many will arrive by the following Friday? Design a book for the shop to record all of the deliveries.

ELG and PNS linked objectives

• FS: Recognize, create and describe patterns (ELG)
• Y1: Describe simple patterns and relationships involving shapes (PNS)
• Y2: Describe patterns and relationships involving shapes, make predictions and test these with examples (PNS)
• Y3: Identify patterns in numbers to solve problems (PNS)

Example 5.2   Shopping bags

Learning context: graphics area

Learning objectives: exploring patterns involving shapes

	FS	Y1	Y2
Activity	Children stick paper clothes silhouettes in a pattern and use joining materials to make a simple 'shopping bag'. Embellish with their own graphics.	Children draw a clothes pattern and embellish it with their own graphics. Make into a simple 'shopping bag'.	As Y1.
Resources	Paper silhouettes of T-shirts, trousers, skirts; writing materials; paper of varying size and colour; sticky tape; hole punch; ribbon.	Writing and drawing materials; paper of varying size and colour; sticky tape; hole punch; ribbon.	As Y1.
Prompt and key questions	The clothes shop needs some new shopping bags. Can you design and make a shopping bag with a repeating clothes pattern on the front? What else can you write on the bag? What pattern have you made? What comes next/ before/in between?	The clothes shop needs some new shopping bags. Can you design and make a shopping bag with a repeating clothes pattern on the front? What type of pattern have you made?	The clothes shop needs some new shopping bags. Can you design and make a shopping bag with different line patterns on the front? What is different about each of the patterns? Can you describe each pattern? How many times have you used the same shape in each pattern?
Key vocabulary	• the same • different • before • after • in between • shape names	• the same • different • before • after • in between • repeating patterns • shape names	• the same • different • repeating pattern • shape names
Opportunities for assessment	• selects paper clothes silhouettes to create sequence and copies this to make a pattern • can describe the pattern using appropriate mathematical language	• draws repeating pattern and is able to describe it using mathematical language • can identify the type of pattern they have made (ABBABB etc.)	• draws repeating patterns • can describe the type of patterns made • can discuss similarities and differences between the patterns with increasing use of mathematical language

Links with Y3: Activity

Design bags with a symmetrical pattern. Which shapes will you choose?

ELG and PNS linked objectives

- FS: Recognize, create and describe patterns (ELG)
- Y1: Describe patterns or relationships involving shapes (PNS)
- Y2: Describe patterns and relationships involving shapes and make predictions (PNS)
- Y3: Identify patterns involving shapes, and use these to solve problems (PNS)

Example 5.3   Price labels for charity clothes shop

Learning context: graphics area

Learning objectives: exploring patterns in numbers

	FS	Y1	Y2
Activity	Children design and make price tags for a clothes shop. Use in the clothes shop and develop related role play.	As FS.	As FS.
Resources	Card; scissors; hole punch; pieces of string; coloured pens/pencils; number line 0–10.	As FS, but include a price list: socks 2p, T-shirts 4p, shorts 6p …	As FS, but include a price list: vests 10p, tights 20p, trousers 40p …
Prompt and key questions	Can you design and make some price tags for the clothes shop? Start at 1p. Each price tag you write must be 1p more than the last one. What do you notice? Can you put them in order? Can you see a pattern in the numbers you have written? Can you talk about what you notice?	Look at the price list in the graphics area. Do you notice a pattern in the prices? Can you design and make some price tags for these values? Can you make more price tags, continuing the pattern you have spotted?	As Y1.
Key vocabulary	<ul><li>number names</li><li>amount</li><li>getting bigger</li><li>more than</li><li>1 more than</li></ul>	<ul><li>amount</li><li>order</li><li>pattern</li><li>even numbers</li><li>increase</li><li>greater than</li></ul>	<ul><li>amount</li><li>order</li><li>increase</li><li>pattern</li><li>doubles</li></ul>
Opportunities for assessment	<ul><li>attempts to write numerals</li><li>writes numerals correctly</li><li>orders prices written correctly</li><li>makes links between values written and number line</li><li>can identify and talk about numbers increasing by 1</li></ul>	<ul><li>writes prices correctly</li><li>can identify and talk about pattern on the price list</li><li>can continue the pattern accurately, calculating what comes next and why</li></ul>	<ul><li>uses £.p notation correctly</li><li>can identify and talk about pattern on the price list</li><li>can continue the pattern accurately, calculating or predicting what comes next and why</li></ul>

Links with Y3: Activity

Some of the price labels have gone missing. Can you spot the pattern and make the missing labels?
92p; 97p; £1.02; £1.07: ____; ____; ____; £1.27; £1.33; ____; ____; ____; £1.57

ELG and PNS linked objectives

- FS: Recognize, create and describe patterns (ELG)
- Y1: Describe patterns and relationships involving numbers; decide whether examples satisfy given conditions (PNS)
- Y2: Describe patterns and relationships involving numbers, make predictions and test these with examples (PNS)
- Y3: Identify patterns in numbers to solve problems (PNS)

Example 5.4   The launderette

Learning context: role play

Learning objectives: exploring patterns involving shapes and numbers

	FS	Y1	Y2
Activity	Children hang laundered clothes on a drying frame in a repeating pattern. They arrange boxes of washing powder and bottles of fabric conditioner in repeating patterns. Develop launderette role play.	As FS.	As FS.
Resources	Selection of T-shirts, socks, scarves for washing; pegs; washing line; washing/drying machine (made out of large boxes); machine 'tokens'; washing baskets; washing powder boxes (empty); fabric conditioner bottles (empty).	As FS.	As FS.
Prompt and key questions	The launderette attendant likes to display things in repeating patterns. Find different ways to display boxes and bottles for sale. How many different ways can you hang up the washing to make different repeating patterns?	As FS.	As FS.
Key vocabulary	<ul><li>the same</li><li>different</li><li>before</li><li>after</li><li>in between</li></ul>	<ul><li>the same</li><li>different</li><li>change</li><li>repeating patterns</li></ul>	<ul><li>the same</li><li>different</li><li>repeating patterns</li></ul>
Opportunities for assessment	<ul><li>selects role-play resources to create a sequence and copies this to make a pattern</li><li>can describe pattern using appropriate mathematical language</li></ul>	<ul><li>can construct a variety of different patterns using a variety of resources</li><li>can describe pattern using appropriate mathematical language</li></ul>	<ul><li>can construct and describe a variety of patterns using different resources</li><li>can interpret and record patterns as ABAB etc.</li></ul>

Links with Y3: Activity

Tokens for the launderette are bought in bags of 5. Can you make enough tokens to fill 7 bags?

ELG and PNS linked objectives

- FS: Recognize, create and describe patterns (ELG)
- Y1: Describe patterns and relationships involving numbers or shapes (PNS)
- Y2: Describe patterns or relationships involving numbers or shapes and make predictions (PNS)
- Y3: Identify patterns in numbers (PNS)

Example 5.5   Button patterns

Learning context: play tray

Learning objectives: exploring patterns involving shapes

	FS	Y1	Y2
Activity	Children design a button layout on clothes by selecting different buttons and laying them in a repeating pattern on clothes silhouettes.	As FS.	As FS.
Resources	Flat (cement-mixing) play tray; a selection of buttons of different shapes, sizes, colours; large clothes silhouettes (card silhouettes of trousers, T-shirts, etc., covered in fabric).	As FS.	As FS.
Prompt and key questions	The clothes being made in the factory need to have buttons on them. Can you choose which buttons you would like to use and lay them in a pattern? What comes next/before/in between? Can you describe your pattern?	The clothes being made in the factory need to have buttons on them, but they must be in a repeating pattern. Can you make one pattern, then think about which type of button you could add or take away to change the pattern. Describe the patterns you have made. What types of pattern are they?	As Y1.
Key vocabulary	• shape names • colours • the same • different • before • after • in between • pattern	• shape names • change • the same • different • repeating pattern	• shape names • repeating patterns
Opportunities for assessment	• selects buttons to create a sequence and copies this to make a pattern • can describe pattern using appropriate mathematical language	• names the shapes used to construct a pattern • can describe the type of pattern (ABAB etc.)	• names the shapes used to construct a pattern • can describe pattern with increasing use of mathematical language

Links with Y3: Activity

Design a garment with arrangements of buttons on the front, such as doubles or multiples of a number. Show a friend and see if they can spot the mathematical pattern.

ELG and PNS linked objectives

- FS: Recognize, create and describe patterns (ELG)
- Y1: Describe patterns and relationships involving shapes (PNS)
- Y2: Describe patterns and relationships involving shapes and make predictions (PNS)
- Y3: Identify patterns in numbers (PNS)

Example 5.6   The market stall

Learning context: role play

Learning objectives: exploring patterns involving shapes and numbers

	FS	Y1	Y2
Activity	Children build a market stall with large wooden bricks or crates. Create a display of clothes to sell in a repeating pattern by laying clothes out in a pattern and/or hanging them in a repeating pattern. Develop role play.	As FS. In addition: children record pictorially the repeating patterns they have made.	As Y1.
Resources	Wooden blocks or crates; washing line or clothes hanging rack; pegs; a selection of small clothes to sell such as scarves, socks, saris; money; purses; shopping bags; writing materials.	In addition to FS: clipboard and writing materials.	As Y1.
Prompt and key questions	The market trader likes to make the clothes stall interesting by displaying clothes for sale in different ways each day. Can you help by finding different repeating patterns? Can you describe your pattern? What comes next/in between/before?	As FS. In addition: How many different patterns have you made? Make a record of the different patterns the trader has used over a week.	As Y1.
Key vocabulary	<ul><li>the same</li><li>different</li><li>next</li><li>before</li><li>in between</li></ul>	<ul><li>the same</li><li>different</li><li>repeating patterns</li></ul>	<ul><li>repeating patterns</li><li>predictions</li><li>result</li></ul>
Opportunities for assessment	<ul><li>selects clothes to make simple sequence and repeats to make a repeating pattern</li><li>describes pattern accurately</li></ul>	<ul><li>constructs different repeating patterns</li><li>can talk about patterns made and identify types of pattern (AABBAABB etc.)</li><li>can record patterns made pictorially</li></ul>	<ul><li>tackles problem in a logical and organized way</li><li>can record repeating patterns</li><li>constructs a variety of patterns and describes what type of pattern they are</li></ul>

Links with Y3: Activity

Make and display price tags in a number pattern. Can the customers work out the pattern?

ELG and PNS linked objectives

- FS: Recognize, create and describe patterns (ELG)
- Y1: Describe patterns and relationships involving numbers or shapes (PNS)
- Y2: Describe patterns and relationships involving numbers or shapes, make predictions and test these with examples (PNS)
- Y3: Identify patterns in numbers (PNS)

6

Shape and space

This chapter covers:

- concepts developed during activities using 3D and 2D shapes
- exploring shapes in the environment
- position and movement in play
- examples of focused teaching activities and recorded work, along with independent activities based on the theme of 'the street'.

Meaningful exploration of shapes is essential for good quality teaching and learning. When children construct a model for a specific purpose, for example, it is their experience and their understanding of the shapes' properties and the shapes' relationships with one another that will inform the decisions and actions they take, not their knowledge of shape names. Children need to have a wide range of experiences with shapes, including:

- drawing around 3D and 2D shapes
- making pictures with 2D shapes
- making models with 3D shapes
- posting shapes through holes
- moving their bodies in and out of structures
- sculpting and decompressing shapes made with malleable materials
- discussing shapes with adults and peers.

These are the very experiences that act as the basis for geometrical analysis at a later stage (Haylock and Cockburn, 2013). It is crucial, therefore, that young children should be stimulated and excited enough to want to 'move shapes around', and have support from practitioners who can model mathematical vocabulary and encourage concept development.

3D shapes

When working with 3D shapes, children will be developing their understanding of:

- the relationship between the faces of a shape and its movement (does it roll or slide?)
- arrangements and packing (can the shape be stacked easily?)
- the shape's properties
- relationships between shapes.

Young children will have spent much of their formative lives engaging with 3D shapes and therefore may well be familiar with their properties, if not their mathematical names. Practitioners therefore need to build on the experiences young children have had with these shapes, and not overlook this in preference for relatively low-quality name-learning activities, such as colouring in pictures of 3D shapes. Children need to manipulate shapes in a wide variety of materials and in different contexts, where mathematical vocabulary is sensitively introduced and modelled, and where children have real reasons to practise using it.

Block play

Both unit and large hollow blocks provide children with the experience of exploring the properties of shape within the context of imaginative play, pursuing their own schematic play and in problem solving (Cubey, 1999; Gura, 1992). While the smaller unit blocks can be used to construct small worlds, the large hollow blocks can be used to create trains, boats, caves and an abundance of other imaginative settings.

Commercial construction kits

Although these kits are prescriptive in terms of possibilities, they allow children to explore a wide range of shapes to fit a specific purpose.

Recyclable materials and modelling dough

Children can assemble and disassemble, stretch and compress, giving them valuable experience at moving aspects of their model to change its function. Working with clay or modelling dough gives children the chance to create a 3D shape they may not yet have the skills to draw, and again allows them to explore how form and function can be changed in this malleable material.

2D shapes

Activities which will help children develop concepts of 2D shapes are:

- making pictures by combining 2D shapes (using shapes themselves, or by drawing around shapes)
- making patterns (see Chapter 5)
- exploring faces of 3D shapes, by manipulating the nets of shapes and printing with the faces
- exploring different thicknesses and orientations of lines through drawing, painting, sewing and collage
- observing and moving shapes, discovering that some shapes do not change their appearance when turned through certain angles (rotational symmetry), and that some shapes look exactly the same on each side when folded (line of symmetry).

Shape in the environment

Our environment, both internal and external, is full of shapes which young children can observe and interact with. Young children and babies, as soon as they are physically able, handle, touch, smell and taste 3D shapes. Studying shapes in the environment provides excellent, imaginative links with geography, literacy and mathematics. Tables 6.1 and 6.2 illustrate realistic links between two popular early years geography-based themes and maths and literacy. School grounds themselves offer an abundance of opportunities to explore shape and space through observing, drawing and replicating a variety of media and model-making features such as buildings, brick patterns, stone, pathways, plants, leaves, fencing, etc.

Shape in art

Once again, works of art provide a stimulus for the exploration of shape, both 2D and 3D work. Sharing works of art can stimulate the use of mathematical vocabulary and inspire children to create their own work, using a variety of media in the style of a particular artist. Particularly useful pieces are by the following artists (see Resources):

- Piet Mondrian
- Andy Goldsworthy
- Auguste Herbin
- Barbara Hepworth
- Wassily Kandinsky.

Position and movement

Activities in which children move artefacts from one point to the next and draw representations of the resultant image will enable them to develop concepts of position (including observing features from different positions), direction and distance.

Table 6.1 Local environment

Geography/Understanding the world	Opportunities for exploring shape and space	Links with literacy
• Carry out fieldwork – go for a shape walk, observing brick/stone work in paths, fencing, buildings, etc.	• Create drawings and collages of patterns and shapes observed.	• *The Big Concrete Lorry* (and other Trotter Street stories) by Shirley Hughes.
• Collect natural materials – leaves, twigs, flowers, shells, pebbles, etc.	• Provide a play tray containing natural materials, magnifying lens and sketching materials. Children observe, sort, sketch materials.	• *Snail Trail* by Ruth Brown.
• Discuss the route from home to school.	• Explore pictorial map making and use of simple coordinates.	• *Traffic Jam* by Annie Owen.
• Carry out a vehicle survey.	• Use construction kits and wooden blocks to build a variety of vehicles.	• Develop traffic role play.
• Create a small-world scene of the local environment. Use geographical language and simple coordinates.	• Use reclaimed materials to construct axels. • Give directions, follow road signs, construct parking bays. • Use positional language and simple coordinates.	• Develop a narrative for small-world play.

Table 6.2 Islands and seasides

Geography/Understanding the world	Opportunities for exploring shape and space	Links with literacy
• Make picture maps of real and imaginary island and seaside scenes. Use appropriate geographical language: island, coastline, hill, dune, sea, ocean, etc.	• Try map making, drawing and positioning shapes. Use positional and spatial language.	• *Come Away From the Water, Shirley* by John Burningham.
• Set up small-world drama/role play using toy and real seaside artefacts.	• Use spatial and positional language.	• *Jack's Fantastic Voyage* by Michael Foreman.
• Carry out fieldwork and collect beach artefacts.	• Provide a play tray filled with beach artefacts for sorting/drawing/imaginary play.	• *Katie Morag and the Two Grandmothers* (and other Katie Morag stories) by Mairi Hedderwick.
	• Create observational drawings and paintings, sculptures and fabric and thread.	• Develop narrative in voyage/ferry boat/pirate role play.

There is huge scope for this type of activity in the early years classroom (some of which is detailed in the Examples later in this chapter). We can begin by considering the main categories of experience.

Small worlds

As seen in Chapter 2, these offer excellent opportunities for linking geography and mathematics. By providing resources that children can manipulate to create roads, enclosures, pathways, bridges, tunnels, oceans, rivers, parking spaces, etc., children can extend their understanding of concepts of shape and space to create small worlds that fit their purpose. Teaching and learning using small worlds can be developed by:

- introducing characters or vehicles that can be moved around the scene in order to give children a purpose for developing a narrative in which positional language is used
- varying the place in which small worlds are set up, sometimes on table-tops (allowing children a good view down onto the scene) and sometimes on the floor (allowing children both to sit around it and to 'get into' the scene)
- involving children in the setting up of a small world, either by following a simple plan or in the retelling of a story or route
- encouraging different children to describe what they see as they sit around a small world. A feature near to one child will be far away from the child sitting opposite, for example, thus enabling them to compare their perspectives and to discuss why their views differ
- encouraging children to draw picture maps of what they see and compare them with those of their peers. Some children have a very keen sense of shape and space and can represent the position and orientation of features very accurately
- by throwing ribbon over the small-world scene and using letter and numeral cards to create simple coordinates which can be used to describe the precise location of a specific feature.

ICT

Concepts of shape and space can be imaginatively and creatively explored by using various forms of ICT (see Activities starting on p.82). Cameras and programmable toys are particularly useful resources to encourage the exploration of shape and space. Activities with cameras can be used to stimulate the use of positional and shape vocabulary, and discussion about how views from different positions can vary by:

- photographing small-world dramas and layouts from different positions
- filming/photographing features in the locality.

Programmable toys will stimulate discussion about movement and directional language. Layouts can be made depicting scenes from stories, while the programmable toy can become a vehicle or character from the story in order to make the activity meaningful. Drawing a grid on the layout enables children to estimate more easily how far the toy needs to travel in order to reach a particular destination and the children can then programme it to follow the required route.

Sculpture and model making

Making sculptures and models using a variety of materials provides children with opportunities to move objects, experiment with positions and use positional language when they discuss their work. Youngsters may be:

- making sculptures on a black cloth on a table or in a cement-mixing tray using a variety of natural and manufactured materials (see Chapter 2)
- using wooden blocks laid out in specific arrangements (circles, spirals, curved or zigzag walls)
- modelling using recyclable materials to cut, disassemble and join
- using clay or modelling dough.

PE

The potential of PE activities in helping to develop a sense of space, position and, importantly, a movement vocabulary should not be underestimated. When children use large apparatus, they will be moving over, under, through, inside, in between and along pathways that might be curved or zigzagged. Dance offers many opportunities for children to hear, interpret and use movement and positional language. Inviting children to move with a variety of props can act to stimulate their own movement and descriptive language. Typical props might be:

- long ribbons
- silk scarves
- plastic mirrors/sheets of reflective paper
- balloons/balls
- bubbles.

Shape and space

flat, curved, straight; round; hollow, solid; corner; point, pointed; face, side, edge, end; surface

3D shapes

cube; cuboid; pyramid; sphere; cone; cylinder

2D shapes

circle, circular; triangle, triangular; square; rectangle, rectangular; pentagon; hexagon; octagon

Direction and movement

around; opposite; corner; angle; clockwise, anti-clockwise; slide; roll; stretch; bend; under; inside, outside; beside; in between; through; towards; next to; left, right; near, far away from; forwards, backwards, sideways; across; direction; turn, half a turn, a quarter turn

Examples of activities

Activity 6.1   Shopping bag

Learning objective:	Exploring features and properties of 3D shapes.
Resources:	A shopping bag containing everyday 3D packaging; plain paper; paint.
How to begin:	Ask the children to unpack the shopping bag and find ways to stack the packages, encouraging them to talk about which shapes will/will not roll as they do so. Use this activity as a means of encouraging the children to discuss the properties of the shapes they are handling. Ask the children to talk about the shape of the items' faces, and to select a particular item, paint each face and print with it on the same large piece of paper.
Development:	Ask the children to describe the prints they have made and encourage other children to identify which package made these prints and ask them to explain their reasoning.
Key vocabulary:	Roll; slide; curved; straight; cube; cuboid; cylinder; round; square; oblong; circle.
Extension:	Using the IWB, display each face of a 3D shape. Encourage the children to discuss what they see and, using their observations and deductions, suggest which shape it might be.

Activity 6.2   Shadow puppets

Learning objective:	Exploring features and properties of 2D shapes.
Resources:	Assorted 2D shapes in black sugar paper; art straws; glue; sticky tape.
How to begin:	Invite the children to use the shapes to make simple vehicles, buildings and street sign shapes that can be used to create a shadow puppet play set in a street. Allow the children time to explore the shapes before selecting which ones they would like to stick together to create their person, vehicle or building. This activity provides opportunities for children to explore the properties of shapes, tessellation and a context for the use of shape vocabulary and mathematical names.
Development:	Once the puppets are made, they should be attached to dowelling. Then, using a large sheet of white cotton as a screen with a projector, or other light source, positioned behind it, the children can develop their play. Use the experience to generate mathematical talk about which shapes were the most popular in the puppet making, which worked best and why.
Key vocabulary:	Curved; straight; round; big; small; square; oblong; circle; semi-circle; triangle.

Activity 6.3   Windows and doors

Learning objectives:	Exploring and visualizing common 2D shapes.
Resources:	IWB; images of local architecture.
How to begin:	Using images of a variety of interesting windows and doors of buildings in the locality, such as those of Mosques and historical buildings, encourage the children to describe the shapes they see. Identify some common 2D shapes within the images such as pentagon, semi-circle, etc.
Development:	Using the draw and reveal facilities of the IWB, gradually reveal one of the shapes discussed. Encourage the children to predict what the shape is and to explain their thinking. Once revealed, discuss whether this shape would make a good window or door and discuss why or why not.
Key vocabulary:	Pentagon; square; circle; semi-circle; arch; triangle; rectangle; straight; curved; long; short.
Extension:	Explain that the children are going to be designers and will need to select shapes carefully to design windows and doors of new buildings. The children can then use a variety of 2D shapes to design windows.

Activity 6.4   The bus journey

Learning objective:	Exploring features and properties of 2D and 3D shapes.
Resources:	Assorted large wooden blocks or plastic crates; dressing-up clothes; card; writing materials.
How to begin:	Ask the children to select wooden blocks or crates to construct a 'bus' so they can travel into town. Encourage the children to talk about which shapes to select and which shapes fit together well. Use this opportunity to model key vocabulary and encourage the children to use it in their mathematical talk. Encourage the children to make sure there are enough seats for each of them.
Development:	Once the bus is constructed, the children might like to make bus tickets and road signs using card and writing materials. Again, this provides opportunities for the children to practise using mathematical language to describe and name 2D shapes, and to explore their properties in a meaningful context. Encourage the children to develop bus journey role play, heightening the profile of the key vocabulary.
Key vocabulary:	Long; short; fits together; flat sides; faces; square; oblong; cube; cuboid.
Extension:	This activity, of course, also lends itself to developing many other mathematical areas, such as:

- estimation and measurement – How long/wide will the bus have to be? Is the bus long enough/wide enough for all of the passengers? How can we measure it?

(Continued)

(Continued)

- counting and calculation – Have we got enough seats for all of the passengers? How can we find out? How many more do we need to make?
- money and calculation – How much does your ticket cost? How can you make that amount? Will you need some change?

As the activity draws on all of these areas, it is advisable for the practitioner to select a main focus for the activity on which to concentrate, while ensuring the other areas are addressed to make the mathematics 'real'.

Principles into practice

- Avoid over-emphasis on name learning, ensuring that children are involved in activities where they are experiencing and discussing the properties of shapes.
- Provide opportunities for children to sculpt shapes with malleable materials, changing them by stretching and compression.
- Explore ways to make links with aspects of the geography and UW to give real purpose for developing positional language and spatial awareness.
- Avoid over-use of commercial regular 2D and 3D shapes, and use 2D and 3D works of art to stimulate the use of mathematical vocabulary, and creative picture and model making.

ICT

Street map

Objective:	use of positional language.
ICT resources:	Apple TV; programmable toys.
Activity:	children film while they program a toy to travel around a street layout outdoors and give spoken directions as they do so. Simultaneously, another group of children watch this on the screen indoors and, listening to the directions, draw the corresponding map of the journey.

2D shape game

Objective:	understanding properties of simple 2D shapes and the language of shape.
ICT resources:	IWB.
Activity:	one member of the group is the 'planner' while the other children choose a simple 2D shape. They then describe it to the 'planner' who follows their descriptions and uses a virtual pen to draw the shape on the IWB. Has the 'planner' drawn the shape correctly? Does the drawn shape resemble the chosen shape? What is the same/different?

Shape quiz

Objective:	using the language of shape.
ICT resources:	video conferencing equipment.

This activity is particularly useful for classes who have already established video links with classes from another school. In one school, children have chosen a particular shape which children from the other school try to identify by asking questions about its properties. Once they have guessed correctly, the shape is revealed on the screen.

Glossary

Rotation: the movement of an object around a fixed point.

Symmetry: a picture or object that has 'sameness' on two sides.

Tessellation: fitting shapes together without leaving gaps.

Translation: movement along a straight line.

UW: understanding the world.

Further reading

Haylock, D. and Cockburn, A. (2013) *Understanding Mathematics for Young Children*, 4th edition. London: Sage Publications. This is a good book for subject knowledge.

Montague-Smith, A. and Price, A.J. (2012) *Mathematics in Early Years Education*. London: Routledge. This text contains a comprehensive chapter on shape and space, including constructing and deconstructing shapes. There is also a chapter on sorting, matching and handling data, suggesting how these skills can be applied.

Examples of independent activities: The street

Example 6.1   Prints in modelling dough

Learning context: malleable materials

Learning objectives: exploring properties and visualizing common 2D shapes and 3D solids

	FS	Y1	Y2
Activity	Children use a selection of items from a 'shopping bag' to print in modelling dough. Children discuss the shape of the prints made and use them to make their own patterns.	As FS.	In addition to FS, children work with a partner who tries to identify the shape whose face has made the print.
Resources	A 'shopping bag' that contains a selection of pasta shapes; cylindrical battery; empty aerosol can; small cuboid and cube packaging; modelling dough.	As FS.	As FS.
Prompt and key questions	Look at the shopping in the bag. What prints do you think they will make in the modelling dough? How are the prints they make different from each other? Can you tell which object made which print? How did you work that out?	As FS.	Look at the items of shopping from the bag. Can you think what shapes their faces will make in the modelling dough? Make some prints and ask a friend to work out which of the items made the print and why.
Key vocabulary	• straight • curved • round • wavy • stretch • bend • circle • square • oblong	• straight • curved • circle • oblong • square • cylinder • cube • cuboid	• straight • curved • circle • oblong • cube • cuboid • regular • irregular
Opportunities for assessment	• can use shape vocabulary to describe properties • uses vocabulary of shape and position to describe prints • can name and identify some simple 2D and 3D shapes	• can use an increasing range of vocabulary to describe shape properties • uses vocabulary of shape and position to describe prints • can name and identify some 2D and 3D shapes	• can use an increasing range of vocabulary to describe shape properties • uses vocabulary of shape and position to describe prints • can name and identify an increasing range of 2D and 3D shapes

Links with Y3: Activity

Model a shape that has reflective symmetry. Cut the shape in half and pass half to a friend to reconstruct.

ELG and PNS linked objectives

• FS: Explore characteristics of everyday objects and shapes and use mathematical language to describe them (ELG)
• Y1: Visualize and name common 2D shapes and 3D solids and describe their features (PNS)
• Y2: Visualize common 2D shapes and 3D solids and identify shapes from pictures of them, referring to their properties (PNS)
• Y3: Draw and complete shapes with reflective symmetry (PNS)

Example 6.2   Kandinsky houses

Learning context: table-top

Learning objective: sorting and arranging 2D shapes referring to their properties

	FS	Y1	Y2
Activity	Children look at and discuss a selection of prints by Kandinsky (or Herbin), using this to inspire making their own pictures with coloured 2D shapes. Children talk about and describe their pictures.	As FS.	As FS.
Resources	A selection of prints by Kandinsky or Herbin; a table covered in black velvet cloth; white cardboard picture frames; assorted coloured 2D shapes.	As FS.	As FS.
Prompt and key questions	Look at the Kandinsky prints and notice the different shapes and colours used. What ideas does it give you? Can you use these ideas to make your own picture of a street scene? Can you describe your picture? What shapes have you used and why? Which shapes fit together and which do not?	As FS.	As FS.
Key vocabulary	• curved • straight • round • circle • bigger than • smaller than • fits together • shape names	• curved • straight • square • oblong • triangle • circle • semi-circle • fits together	• area • curved • straight • tessellation • circle • semi-circle • square • oblong • pentagon • hexagon
Opportunities for assessment	• can use vocabulary of shape and position to describe a picture • can observe and discuss similarities and differences between shapes • can identify and name simple 2D shapes	• can use vocabulary of shape and position to describe a picture • can observe and discuss similarities and differences between a variety of simple 2D shapes • can identify and name an increasing range of simple 2D shapes	• can use an increasing range of mathematical language to describe a picture • can identify, name and talk about the properties of an increasing range of 2D shapes

Links with Y3: Activity

Use a set square to draw shapes with right angles on coloured paper. Cut them out and arrange them to make a picture in the style of Kandinsky. How do the shapes tessellate?

ELG and PNS linked objectives

- FS: Explore characteristics of everyday objects and shapes and use mathematical language to describe them (ELG)
- Y1: Visualize and name common 2D shapes and use them to make pictures (PNS)
- Y2: Sort, make and describe 2D shapes, referring to their properties (PNS)
- Y3: Use a set square to draw right angles and identify right angles in 2D shapes (PNS)

Example 6.3   View from a hot air balloon

Learning context: small-world drama

Learning objectives: using positional language to talk about direction and movement, and giving instructions

	FS	Y1	Y2
Activity	Children engage with a small-world drama of a town scene, countryside and coastline. Children develop a narrative of travellers in the hot air balloon, describing what they can see below as they fly over the scene.	As FS.	As FS.
Resources	Green, brown, blue drapes; small wooden houses/buildings; assorted vehicles and road signs; play people; a selection of farm animals; stones, bark, twigs (to construct animal enclosures); boats; sea animals; hot air balloon (made from papier mache over a balloon, and yoghurt pot suspended from it).	As FS.	As FS, plus clipboard and writing materials.
Prompt and key questions	The travellers are flying over a town. Can you be a traveller and describe what you see to your companion? What lies below you? What is in front of/behind you? What is nearest to you/further away?	As FS.	The travellers are travelling over a town. They need to find the most interesting route over the countryside and town and to the coast. Talk to your companion about the most interesting route and write or draw instructions for other travellers to follow.
Key vocabulary	• on top • underneath • beside • near • far • next to • turn	• underneath • above • near • turn • opposite • right • left • between • middle	• underneath • below • opposite • turn • right • left • between • middle
Opportunities for assessment	• can use positional language to describe a journey	• can use positional language with increasing accuracy to describe a journey	• can use positional language with increasing accuracy to describe a journey • can represent a small-world scene accurately in a drawing

Links with Y3: Activity

One group of children plans a journey for the hot air balloon, writing instructions. A second group follows the instructions using a compass.

ELG and PNS linked objectives

- FS: Use everyday language to talk about position (ELG)
- Y1: Use everyday language to describe the position of objects and direction and distance when moving them (PNS)
- Y2: Follow and give instructions involving position, direction and movement (PNS)
- Y3: Read and record vocabulary of position, direction and movement about a grid (PNS)

Example 6.4   Symmetrical shapes

Learning context: play tray

Learning objective: using everyday words to describe how shapes turn about a point or line

	FS	Y1	Y2
Activity	Children explore line symmetry by holding mirrors alongside a selection of half pictures. They explore moving the mirror across the pictures in different ways until the reflection completes the image. Children discuss the shapes and images they see.	As FS, but children also make their own symmetrical drawings to investigate with the mirror.	As Y1.
Resources	6 half pictures; 2 small, flat plastic mirrors.	In addition to FS: paper and drawing materials.	As Y1.
Prompt and key questions	How do the pictures change when you hold the mirror against them? Can you describe what you see? As you move the mirror over the picture, where is the mirror when the picture and reflection make the whole shape? What do you notice?	In addition to FS: Can you make your own symmetrical drawing? What happens when you hold the mirror alongside?	As Y1.
Key vocabulary	• longer • shorter • reflection • the same • whole • complete • upwards • downwards • turn	• the same • reflection • symmetrical	• reflection • symmetrical • line of symmetry
Opportunities for assessment	• uses mathematical vocabulary to describe activity • recognizes and identifies when reflection creates the whole picture	• uses mathematical vocabulary to describe activity • can identify the symmetrical nature of the pictures • can create own simple symmetrical picture	• can recognize and identify the symmetrical nature of the pictures • uses vocabulary of symmetry and reflection • can create own simple symmetrical picture

Links with Y3: Activity

Children draw their own shapes, cut them in half and pass to a friend to complete.

ELG and PNS linked objectives

- FS: Use everyday language to talk about position (ELG)
- Y1: Identify shapes that turn about a point or line (PNS)
- Y2: Identify reflective symmetry in patterns and 2D shapes (PNS)
- Y3: Draw and complete shapes with reflective symmetry; draw the reflection of a shape in a mirror along one side (PNS)

Example 6.5   Sorting parcels

Learning context: role play

Learning objectives: sorting 3D solids, describing their features and referring to their properties, identifying 3D solids from pictures of them

	FS	Y1	Y2
Activity	Children discuss and sort a variety of parcels into labelled sacks. Children develop Post Office role play.	As FS.	As FS, but children also record how many of each shape of parcel have been sorted.
Resources	Assorted wrapped parcels including cubes, cuboids and cylinders; 3 large sacks of each corresponding shape name: 'cube' 'cuboid' and 'cylinder'; writing materials; typical dressing-up clothes and Post Office resources.	As FS.	As FS.
Prompt and key questions	The Post Office workers need to sort the parcels into sacks. Look carefully at the shapes of the parcels and find ways to sort them into the sacks. How have you sorted the parcels? What is the same/different about the parcels? Which shapes have flat/curved faces? Which shapes roll? Why?	The Post Office workers need to sort the parcels into sacks. Look carefully at the labels on the sacks and sort the parcels into the correct sacks. Can you describe the parcels you need to a friend? What are the differences and similarities between the shapes? Which shapes have flat/curved faces? Which shapes roll? Why?	The Post Office workers need to sort the parcels into sacks and make a record of how many of each shape of parcel they have sorted. Can you sort the parcels into the correct sack and find a way of keeping a record for the manager when the Post Office closes? What information does your record give us about the parcels?
Key vocabulary	<ul><li>straight</li><li>curved</li><li>edge</li><li>face</li><li>roll</li><li>slide</li><li>square</li></ul>	<ul><li>straight</li><li>curved</li><li>circle</li><li>oblong</li><li>cube</li><li>cuboid</li><li>cylinder</li></ul>	<ul><li>circle</li><li>oblong</li><li>cube</li><li>cuboid</li><li>cylinder</li></ul>
Opportunities for assessment	<ul><li>uses shape vocabulary to describe properties</li><li>selects, uses and explains criteria used to sort the parcels</li><li>identifies and names some 2D and 3D shapes</li></ul>	<ul><li>uses shape vocabulary to describe properties</li><li>can relate solid shapes to pictures of them</li><li>identifies and names some 2D and 3D shapes</li></ul>	<ul><li>can relate solid shapes to pictures of them</li><li>identifies and names cube, cuboid and cylinder</li><li>designs a simple means of recording the number of parcels sorted and can talk about the information it shows</li></ul>

Links with Y3: Activity

Using a sheet of images of a selection of 3D shapes, complete a checklist at the Post Office by counting and recording how many parcels there are of each shape.

ELG and PNS linked objectives

- FS: Explore characteristics of everyday objects and shapes and use mathematical language to describe them (ELG)
- Y1: Visualize and name common 3D solids and describe their features (PNS)
- Y2: Identify 3D solids, from pictures of them in different positions and sort and describe, referring to their properties (PNS)
- Y3: Relate 3D solids to drawings of them; describe and classify them (PNS)

Example 6.6   Silhouette Street

Learning context: role play

Learning objective: visualizing, making and describing common 2D shapes

	FS	Y1	Y2
Activity	Children select an envelope from the play tray and hold it up to a light source. They describe and identify the silhouette they see. Children develop a narrative around the silhouettes they see and describe the 'journey' they take down the street.	As FS.	As Y1, with an increasing use of mathematical vocabulary.
Resources	Six sealed envelopes each containing a black sugar paper silhouette of a building with differently shaped cut-out windows.	As FS.	In addition to FS: clipboard and writing materials.
Prompt and key questions	These letters have been posted without an address. You can find out which building they are going to by holding them up to the light. Can you describe the buildings you see? Are the windows the same? What is the same/different about them? Which shapes are curved and which are straight?	As FS.	Can you describe the buildings in order to a friend? Can your friend draw them accurately following your description? Can you make up a story about travelling along this route?
Key vocabulary	• big • small • straight • curved • number names • square • circle • triangle • oblong	• straight • curved • square • oblong • circle • triangle • semi-circle • hexagon • pentagon	• square • oblong • triangle • circle • semi-circle • hexagon • pentagon • area • perimeter
Opportunities for assessment	• uses shape vocabulary to describe building silhouettes • identifies and names a variety of 2D shapes	• uses shape vocabulary to describe building silhouettes • identifies and accurately names a variety of 2D shapes	• uses shape vocabulary to describe building silhouettes accurately • can name and discuss the properties of an increasing number of 2D shapes

Links with Y3: Activity

Using photos of interesting buildings and features in the locality as a stimulus, children draw the silhouettes of buildings on black paper ready for the play trays. Can you relate the silhouette to any of the photos?

ELG and PNS linked objectives

- FS: Explore characteristics of everyday objects and shapes and use mathematical language to describe them (ELG)
- Y1: Visualize and name common 2D shapes and describe their features (PNS)
- Y2: Make and describe 2D shapes, referring to their properties (PNS)
- Y3: Relate 2D shapes to drawings of them; draw and make the shapes (PNS)

7

Measurement

This chapter covers:

- the progression of developing skills and concepts in measuring length
- the terms 'weight' and 'mass'
- imaginative ideas for measuring volume and capacity
- exploring area and perimeter in play
- using time in a playful context
- examples of focused teaching activities and recorded work, along with independent activities based on the theme of 'pets'.

Arguably, measurement in all its forms is the aspect of mathematics that children have had most experience of prior to starting school. In their play and daily activities, children are continually estimating and making comparisons of weight, length, area, time and capacity. They will fill a cup with liquid, find a space big enough to lay out a road mat, and mix powder paint to make a specific colour, all of which involve estimating and comparing amounts for the purpose of solving a problem. As children's skills and understanding of concepts develop, measuring will increasingly involve counting accurately, number operations and selecting and using appropriate measuring equipment. Practitioners need to ensure that the learning environment offers many opportunities for creative and spontaneous uses of measuring, which are supported and consolidated by focused teaching activities. Much of the volume and capacity work that is conducted in Key Stage 1 classrooms (5 to 7 years), for example, involves pouring sand and water when it is in fact possible to use a wide range of other materials that might hold more interest and relevance for young children (see Chapter 2), such as harvesting and cooking fruit and vegetables grown at the setting, or using resources related to a theme or book.

Creative ideas for good practice

Rosie's Walk by Pat Hutchins (see Resources) provides many opportunities for measurement in a small-world layout of the story:

- finding the distance Rosie travels from one feature to the next (length)
- counting the number of toy sheep it would take to cover a field, or the number of toy ducks needed to cover the pond (area)

- measuring the length of fencing required to go around the farmyard (perimeter)
- using a sand timer to find the time taken for a programmable toy to travel around a specific route (time)

and in a play tray:

- using a sand timer to find the time taken to fill a small hessian sack with corn (time and capacity)
- finding the heaviest and lightest bags of corn/flour (weight).

It must be recognized that no measurement is 100 per cent accurate, no matter what type of measurement is being undertaken or what measuring equipment is being used. All measurements involve a degree of rounding up or down. This provides a useful discussion point with older Key Stage 1 children.

When engaged in activities exploring length, weight, volume and capacity from the Foundation Stage through Key Stage 1, children will be developing the following skills and concepts:

- descriptive language
- measuring by comparison and using related language
- ordering objects by quantity
- counting accurately
- using and applying number operations
- using place value
- selecting and using appropriate measuring equipment.

Length

Children have much experience of measuring and estimating length in their play, such as finding blankets, toy fencing, construction pieces, dolls clothes, and painting/ sculpting lines that are long or short enough to fit their purpose. Children's conceptual development of measuring length often develops by:

- comparison, discovering that the two ends of the wooden blocks they are comparing need to be held together in order to measure with any degree of accuracy
- selecting non-standard units, such as books, pencils, blocks, number lines, etc., laying them end to end and counting how many items they have used. This is a very valuable stage owing to the assessment opportunities it gives, and the valuable mathematical discussion it generates
- selecting a uniform non-standard unit such as same-sized bricks
- using a standard unit.

> ### Creative ideas for good practice
>
> Using a small-world floor layout of *Rosie's Walk* for a mixed-age group class:
>
> - Ask some children to measure the distance Rosie travels on her journey from the haycock to the beehive by filling in the space with selected non-standard units. Some children may notice that results depend on the length of the item chosen, contributing to the realization of the need for a uniform unit.
> - Ask some children to suggest a uniform unit they can use to measure the distance such as same-sized wooden bricks, Unifix® cubes, and so on. This useful intermediate stage, avoiding going straight to centimetres, provides children with measuring equipment they can easily handle and further opportunities to realize the need for a standard unit. If everyone chooses a different set of bricks to measure with, the results will not be the same and this heightens awareness of the need for standard units.
> - Ask some children to measure the distance using standard units, selecting unit and measuring equipment appropriately.

Weight

In their play, children will determine the heaviest item by holding and comparing objects and need opportunities to develop appropriate vocabulary such as: heavy, heaviest, heavier than; light, lightest and lighter than. Important points to consider when teaching are:

- Children should be encouraged to describe their findings in complete sentences and, importantly, to say the reciprocal, such as 'The blue bag of treasure is heavier than the red bag. The red bag is lighter than the blue bag'.
- It can be difficult to make true comparisons of weight using a flat hand, so it is beneficial to have objects or materials in bags for the children to hold and compare. For focused teaching activities, the practitioner can have pre-prepared bags (filled with any suitable material) in the guise of theme-related items.
- Weight and mass are two distinct measurements. When children are finding out which object is heaviest by comparison with another object, they are determining the weight of the object, but when they are measuring using another object as a counterbalance, in a bucket balance for example, they are in fact determining the mass of the object.
- The mass of a specific object can be determined using a bucket balance by:

  o finding other objects that counterbalance
  o using uniform non-standard units such as Unifix® cubes to counterbalance
  o progressing to gram masses to counterbalance and provide a standard unit of measurement.

In their chapter on measures, Haylock and Cockburn (2013) suggest important points for practitioners to consider, three of which are summarized as follows:

- Practitioners should be consistent with their use of language, referring to counterbalances used as masses, and not weights.
- Young children's weighing activities should mainly involve the use of balance-type apparatus.
- Practitioners should model and encourage children to use the language 'weighs the same as' when the word weigh is used, for example 'The sack of corn weighs the same as 20g' or 'The sack of corn has a mass of 20g'. This acts to emphasize the equivalence that has emerged.

As well as focused teaching sessions, children should have available to them bucket balances and a variety of resources to use as counterbalances in their play. These should be particularly relevant to role play, both indoors and outdoors (see Chapter 2).

Creative ideas for good practice

- Bags of 'treasure' (velvet bags tied with ribbon).
- Bags of 'corn', 'flour', 'porridge', 'oats' (small tied hessian sacks).
- Bags of 'potting compost', 'cement', 'sand' (small, thick, plastic sacks, thoroughly taped, with a handle).

Area and perimeter

These aspects of measurement are not commonly explored in early years education, but are often a feature of children's play. Children are accustomed to finding out how many things can cover a space, or surround a designated area. For example, in small-world play, children might ask:

- How many cars will fill the car park space?
- How many buildings will fill the building plot?
- How will the railway layout need to go to fit on the table?
- How many pieces of fencing are needed to go around the pond?

In role play and in the outside play area, they might consider:

- How many people can sit on the mat?
- Which sheet covers the cot mattress?
- How many wooden blocks are needed to build a wall around the house?
- How many books cover the surface of the table?
- How many plates cover the tablecloth?
- How many children can stand around the circle?

Practitioners should use the vocabulary of area and perimeter with children during their play and in focused teaching activities when the opportunity arises.

> ☼ Creative ideas for good practice
>
> Children can explore the relationship between constant perimeter and changing area by:
>
> - making enclosures for small-world animals with thick string, discovering that although the length of string remains the same, the enclosure will hold a different number of sheep depending on how it is arranged
> - making parking areas in the outside play area with blocks, discovering that 10 wooden blocks, for example, can be arranged in different ways to make parking spaces that hold different numbers of vehicles.

Volume and capacity

Volume is the 3D space an object occupies, while capacity is the amount a container holds. Much of the capacity work undertaken by children in early years settings involves the pouring of sand and water into different sorts of containers. As seen in Chapter 2, there are a variety of other materials that can be poured successfully. Adding colour to water and providing unusual containers can make capacity work more exciting for children, and help make it more relevant to their interests.

> ☼ Creative ideas for good practice
>
> - Pouring 'milk' – white water (a small amount of white powder paint).
> - Making 'jelly' – water with red food colouring; jelly moulds of differing shapes and sizes; jug.
> - Pouring pirates' 'grog' – brown water (a small amount of brown powder paint); jugs and 'tankards' (either real or plastic beakers covered in tin foil).
> - Making a swamp – green food dye added to water; flour; jugs and bottles of graduated sizes.
> - Making 'gloop cake' – corn flour; water; food colouring; jugs and graduated cake tins.
> - Pouring a 'magic potion' – food colouring; soap flakes (to give a pearlized effect); glitter; jugs and interestingly shaped bottles (bubble bath, shampoo bottles, etc.).

Volume can be explored through model making using commercial construction kits, wooden blocks and recycled materials. 'Parcel sets' can be made by practitioners (by collecting interesting shaped packaging and covering in bright durable paper) and used in relation to themes or stories where presents are exchanged.

Time

When children are working with time, they will:

- use mathematical and historical language (before; next; after; tomorrow; yesterday; last week; next week; etc.)
- sequence events
- compare different units of time

- count
- use number operations
- select and use appropriate measuring equipment.

Children will be aware of time in their everyday experiences: the length of time from one birthday to the next, who is older or younger, the changes in a younger sibling, etc. They may also be involved in different activities on different days and notice changes in their environment with the passing of the seasons. As young children are so often concerned with the present, practitioners should encourage them to be aware of the order of the events in the learning environment by:

- using a visual timetable (displaying agreed symbols to represent events and activities during the day)
- encouraging children to sequence activities, such as cooking or model making, in the form of a simple flow diagram
- sequencing the events in a story or rhyme
- drawing attention (when appropriate) to the shape of the clock hands at specific times of the day: snack time, lunchtime, home time, etc.

Providing equipment for measuring time in role play enables children to practise skills by:

- writing down times/using clock faces to show the opening/closing times of a shop
- measuring the time a washing cycle takes in the launderette
- using a calendar to book holidays/doctor/hair appointments
- writing times on departure tickets
- recording times in log/appointment books.

In a mixed Foundation Stage and Key Stage 1 class (4–7 years), it is particularly important to ensure there is a clear progression of equipment available for children to select and use independently, ensuring that time rockers, sand timers, clocks and stop watches are on hand so that children can select equipment that matches their level of skill, understanding and appropriateness to the task. Children should also be encouraged to measure time intervals and not just read the time.

Length

long; short; tall; high; low; wide; narrow; deep; shallow; thick; thin; depth; width; longer, longer than, longest; shorter, shorter than, shortest; taller, taller than, tallest; higher, higher than, highest; further, further than, furthest; far; near; close

Weight and mass

weighs the same as; balances; heavy; light, lighter than, lightest; heavier, heavier than, heaviest; kilogram, half a kilogram, gram; mass

---

Capacity

full, half full; empty; holds, holds the same as; contains, container

Time

days of the week; months of the year; seasons; today, yesterday, tomorrow; before, after; next, last; now; soon; early; late; quick, quicker, quickest, quickly; fast, faster, fastest; slow, slower, slowest, slowly; old, older, oldest; new, newer, newest; takes longer, takes less time; how long ago?; how long will it be to …?; how long will it take to …?; hour; minute; second; o'clock; half past; quarter to; quarter past; clock; watch; hands; digital/analogue; clock/watch; timer

---

Examples of activities

Activity 7.1   The vet's day

Learning objective:	Use and understanding of the vocabulary of time.
Resources:	Writing materials; analogue clock face (or pictures of the given times); A4 sheets for the appointment book; vet role-play resources.
How to begin:	Following discussion about vets' work and related role play, discuss with the children the sorts of activities the vet might undertake during the day, using opportunities to introduce key vocabulary. Ask the children to draw pictures of the vet involved in various activities during the day. Encourage the children to discuss the events and the time of day they might occur, prompting the use of key vocabulary.
Development:	Ask the children to sequence the pictures, describing when in the day they might occur.
Key vocabulary:	First; before; next; after; later; last; then; morning; afternoon; o'clock and half past times.
Extension:	Ask the children to complete pages in the 'appointment' book, to write down some appointments timed to o'clock or half past times, and write down or draw the nature of the appointment. Use this to stimulate further role play.

I am having breakfast in the morning.   I am going to work.   I am opening the surgery.   I am having lunch at lunchtime.

Figure 7.1   Nadine (R) can sequence familiar events

6 ocloc brexfust

9 ocloc fed the hulst

11 ocloc luch

12 ocloc giv the cat a unjexun

ruffost 8 te bum

Zac was able to record the
times and use them in the
'appointment book'.

Figure 7.2 Zac (Y2) can use and record time

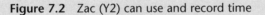

Activity 7.2   Animal blanket

Learning objective:	Heightening of awareness of the need for a uniform unit.
Resources:	Basket of same-sized and differently sized soft toys; small same-sized hand towel for each child.
How to begin:	Explain that the vet has some new blankets for the animals to sit on and they need to find out how many animals can sit on each blanket. Encourage the children to discuss how they might calculate this using the soft toys. This provides the opportunity for the children to cover their 'blanket' in soft toys selected from the basket. Ask the children to count how many toys cover the whole of the blanket, using this opportunity to introduce key words. Compare results and encourage a discussion about why some children will have different results even though their 'blankets' are identical in size. This activity not only allows the children to compare and discuss size and area, but also helps to heighten their awareness of the importance of units chosen in determining an accurate and reliable result.
Development:	Following discussion, ask the children to find out how many animals they will need to cover the 'blanket' if the same-sized animals are used, again modelling and encouraging the use of key vocabulary.
Key vocabulary:	Cover; space; area; all over; more than; less than; equal numbers; number names.
Extension:	Children calculate the area accurately using uniform bricks, envelopes, Numicon® plates, etc.

Activity 7.3   Bird food

Learning objective:	Exploration of volume and equivalence.
Resources:	Play tray; selection of differently shaped containers; funnels; 500ml measuring cylinders (1 per child); bird seed or similar small grain.
How to begin:	This activity focuses on exploring volume and its conservation (or equivalence) when the seed is transferred from one container to another. The pet shop assistant is measuring amounts of bird seed to package and sell. Encourage the children to fill and pour the seed using the differently shaped containers. Introduce and model key vocabulary. Ask the children whether they think the containers hold the same or different volumes of seed.
Development:	Extend the children's discussion and estimation of volume. Introduce the 500ml cylinders. Ask the children to fill carefully a 500ml cylinder and encourage discussion about how the cylinders look the same and hold the same volume. Then ask the children to choose one of the differently shaped containers and pour the seed from their 500ml cylinder into the container. Encourage the children to discuss their observations about how the amount of seed in each container looks different. This will heighten their awareness of equivalence in that the volume of seed has remained the same, although it looks different in all the differently shaped containers.
Key vocabulary:	Empty; full; half full; language of shape and size; volume; space it takes up.
Extension:	Introduce the unit of millilitres and encourage the children to measure accurately the volume 500ml (equivalent to 500cm^3) and further explore conservation.

Activity 7.4   Snake lengths

Learning objective:	Understanding of the need for standard units.
Resources:	Paper, scissors, metre sticks.
How to begin:	Using pet shop role play as a stimulus, for example, suggest that the children make a picture of snakes, or another long creature, for display in the role-play area. Ask the children to suggest how long the snakes might be, for example 6 pencils long. Provide the children with strips of paper and ask them to cut them to the agreed length. Before the children paint them, ask them to compare their lengths with one another and discuss what they notice. This provides them with an opportunity to notice that although they have all worked to an agreed length, their paper snakes will vary, to some extent, in length. Encourage discussion about why this

	may be and use this as an opportunity to introduce standard units.
Development:	Ask the children to measure further strips of paper to an agreed standard length, such as 1 metre, and compare and discuss the results. Paint and display the snakes.
Key vocabulary:	Longer than; shorter than; equal lengths; standard unit; metre; centimetres.

Principles into practice

- Allow young children time to use non-standard units for measuring (books, pencils, bricks, etc.) as they are more likely to be familiar with the required vocabulary, and the objects are probably easier to manipulate than standard units. This gives real opportunities for children to become aware of the need for standard units.
- Avoid meaningless measuring: children are more likely to be enthusiastic about measuring something that holds real meaning for them.
- Vary the materials used for volume and capacity work to maintain interest and relevance.
- Use balance equipment to measure the mass of objects.
- Be consistent with mathematical vocabulary used for weight and mass, such as 'the bag weighs the same as 20 cubes'.

ICT

How high?

Objective:	measuring accurately with standard units.
ICT resources:	Dartfish software (see Resources); laptop; projector.
Activity:	children devise a simple bouncing ball game for dogs. Using the software, children can measure exactly how high the ball has bounced by measuring it in the recorded frames, and therefore find out which child has bounced the ball the highest.

Designing pet homes

Objective:	measuring length with non-standard units.
ICT resources:	visualizer; laptop; projector.
Activity:	children design a cage for a chosen animal. The dimensions are compared on the screen for the children to see and are measured with non-standard units such as small cubes.

Best habitat

Objective:	measuring temperature using standard units.
ICT resources:	datalogger (see Resources).
Activity:	having identified a specific small mammal as the 'research pet', the children investigate which part of the school and school grounds might be most suitable for the animal to live in by using the datalogger to record the temperature of each area. The children compare the recorded results.

Further reading

Haylock, D. and Cockburn, A. (2013) *Understanding Mathematics for Young Children*, 4th edition. London: Sage Publications. This text provides thorough subject knowledge for those teaching 3–8-year-olds.

Newell, K. (2012) *Belair: Early Years – Shape, Space and Measures: Ages 3–5*. Glasgow: Collins Educational. This publication provides lots of practical examples of activities and displays and their relationship with other areas of learning.

Skinner, C. and Stevens, J. (2013) *Foundations of Mathematics: An Active Approach to Number, Shape and Measures in the Early Years*. London: Bloomsbury. This book gives practical ideas for shape, space and measures.

Examples of independent activities: Pets

Example 7.1   Weighing dog biscuits

Learning context: play tray

Learning objective: comparing, estimating and weighing objects using mathematical language

	FS	Y1	Y2
Activity	Children pour and scoop dog biscuits, filling and emptying small hessian sacks. Children explore and discuss whose bag is the heaviest.	As FS, but children use a bucket balance to find the amount of dog biscuits that weighs the same as 20 cubes.	As Y1, but finding bags that weigh the same as 1 kg.
Resources	Assorted dog biscuits; small hessian sacks of different sizes; plastic scoops.	In addition to FS: bucket balance; 20 cubes.	In addition to FS: bucket balance; 1 kg mass.
Prompt and key questions	The pet shop keeper needs to fill the sacks with dog biscuits. Can you help and find out which sack is the heaviest? How can you find out? Do any of the sacks feel as if they weigh the same? Can you put the sacks in order of weight?	The pet shop keeper needs to bag up the dog biscuits. Each bag needs to weigh the same as 20 cubes. What will you do to find the mass of the bags? How do you know each bag weighs the same as 20 cubes?	The pet shop keeper needs to bag up the dog biscuits. Each bag must weigh the same as 1 kg. Can you estimate how many biscuits you will need? What will you do to find the mass accurately? Was your estimate accurate?
Key vocabulary	• heavy • light • heavier than • lighter than • weighs the same as	• heavier than • lighter than • too heavy • too light • weighs the same as • equal • balance • mass	• too heavy • too light • weighs the same as • equal • balance • mass • estimate • accurate • kilogram
Opportunities for assessment	• can use mathematical vocabulary of weight to explain reasoning • can identify accurately which bag is heavier/ lighter than a given weight • can compare weights of two bags • can order more than two bags by weight	• uses mathematical vocabulary to explain • can use bucket balance appropriately • can measure weight with a degree of accuracy	• can use mathematical vocabulary with increasing competence • can give a sensible estimate • can use mathematical apparatus appropriately

Links with Y3 Activity

5 kg of dog biscuits arrive at the pet shop and they will be sold in bags of 500g. Estimate how many dog biscuits will weigh 500g, weigh them and fill bags with 500g of biscuits. How many bags will you need to fill? Keep a record of your results.

ELG and PNS linked objectives

- FS: Use everyday language to talk about weight and to compare objects (ELG)
- Y1: Estimate, weigh and compare objects, choosing and using uniform non-standard units and measuring instruments (PNS)
- Y2: Estimate, compare and measure weights choosing and using standard units and measuring instruments (PNS)
- Y3: Know the relationship between kilograms and grams and choose appropriate units to estimate, measure and record results (PNS)

Example 7.2   Filling animal water bottles

Learning context: play tray

Learning objectives: using everyday language, estimating, measuring and comparing objects, choosing and using suitable uniform non-standard units

	FS	Y1	Y2
Activity	Children pour water and fill and empty animal water bottles. Discuss and compare the capacities of the bottles.	Children pour water and fill and empty water bottles. They count how many jugs of water it takes to fill each bottle.	Children estimate and explore how many water bottles can be filled using a 1 litre measuring jug.
Resources	Selection of differently sized animal water bottles (600 ml, 100 ml, 350 ml, etc.); small jugs.	As FS.	Four 250 ml water bottles; two 500 ml water bottles; 1 litre measuring jug; clipboard and writing materials.
Prompt and key questions	The pet shop keeper needs to fill the water bottles for the animals. Can you help to fill them and find out which bottle holds the most water, and which bottle holds the least? How can you find out? Which water bottle would be best for a mouse? Why? Which would be best for a big rabbit? Why?	The pet shop keeper needs to fill the water bottles for the animals and find out exactly how much water each bottle holds. Can you find a way to work this out? What are your results? Which bottle held the most and which the least? How much more water did the largest bottle hold compared to the smallest?	The pet shop keeper needs to find out how many water bottles can be filled using 1 litre of water. Estimate how many bottles you think 1 litre will fill and then find out. Can you find a way to record your results? What do your results show?
Key vocabulary	• more • less • most • least • empty • full • nearly full • the same amount • enough • not enough	• more • less • full • almost full • empty • half full • more than • less than • equal amounts • the same as	• full • half full • almost full • quarter full • empty • estimate • litres
Opportunities for assessment	• can use mathematical vocabulary of capacity to describe activity • can compare capacities of two containers • can compare and order capacities of more than two containers	• uses mathematical vocabulary of capacity to describe activity • can measure capacity of bottles and talk about results	• uses mathematical vocabulary of capacity with increasing competence • can give a sensible estimate • can measure and talk about capacity of the bottles

Links with Y3 Activity

As Y2. Do you notice a pattern/ relationship in the results?

ELG and PNS linked objectives

• FS: Use everyday language to talk about weight and to compare objects (ELG)
• Y1: Estimate, measure and compare objects, choosing and using suitable uniform non-standard units (PNS)
• Y2: Estimate, compare and measure capacities choosing and using standard units (PNS)
• Y3: Know the relationship between litres and millilitres and choose appropriate units to estimate, measure and record results (PNS)

Example 7.3   Homes for snakes and lizards

Learning context: small world drama

Learning objective: using everyday language to estimate, compare and measure lengths of objects

	FS	Y1	Y2
Activity	Children use a selection of materials to make enclosures that are long enough for a chosen plastic creature. Children develop small world play in which key vocabulary is used.	In addition to FS, children make several enclosures of different lengths and sort creatures into them according to their length. Children develop small world play in which key vocabulary is used.	Children select a creature they estimate to be about 10 cm long. They use materials to construct an enclosure long enough for it. Children develop small world play in which key vocabulary is used.
Resources	Green fabric; stones; pebbles; bark; 'pond' (card covered in silver paper); plastic snakes, newts, lizards of varying lengths.	As FS.	As FS.
Prompt and key questions	The tank in the pet shop has several different creatures who need to have some enclosures made for them. Choose one of the creatures and make a home for it. The home must be long enough. How can you make sure it is long enough? How can you check?	The tank in the pet shop has several creatures of different lengths. They need to have some creatures made for them. Can you make 3 enclosures of different lengths and sort the creatures into them? How can you make sure they are the right length? How can you check? How many creatures are there in each enclosure?	The pet shop keeper needs to make some enclosures for the creatures in the tank. Can you help by estimating which creatures are about 10 cm long and make an enclosure long enough for them? How many creatures do you think are about 10 cm long? How could you check?
Key vocabulary	• longer than • shorter than • narrower • thicker • wider • about the same • too short • too long • not long enough	• longer than • shorter than • narrower • wider • too short • too long • not long enough • equal lengths	• longer than • shorter than • estimate • centimetres
Opportunities for assessment	• can use mathematical vocabulary of length • can compare two lengths • can compare more than two lengths	• uses mathematical vocabulary of length correctly • can compare more than two lengths • can sort for length	• uses mathematical vocabulary of length with increasing confidence • can make sensible estimates

Links with Y3 Activity

Design some cages for the snakes and lizards that are 8 cm x 19 cm; 12 cm x 25 cm; 16 cm x 27 cm. Draw them accurately. Use a visualizer to share them with the class/group.

ELG and PNS linked objectives

- FS: Use everyday language to talk about size and to compare objects (ELG)
- Y1: Estimate, measure and compare objects (PNS)
- Y2: Estimate, compare and measure lengths choosing and using standard units and measuring instruments (PNS)
- Y3: Know the relationship between metres and centimetres and choose appropriate units to estimate, measure and record results (PNS)

Example 7.4   Making a rabbit cage

Learning context: construction area

Learning objectives: using everyday language to estimate, compare and measure lengths of objects

	FS	Y1	Y2
Activity	Children construct a simple cage with Lasy® construction kit which is big enough for a soft toy rabbit to fit into.	As FS, but children estimate how long the cage is and then measure in cubes.	As Y1, but children estimate the length the cage needs to be in centimetres, then measure the constructed cage with a ruler to the nearest centimetre.
Resources	Lasy® construction kit; small soft toy rabbit.	In addition to FS: small uniform cubes.	In addition to FS: centimetre ruler.
Prompt and key questions	The pet shop keeper needs to make a new cage for a rabbit. Can you help by making a cage long enough and wide enough for the rabbit to fit into? What will you need to do to make sure the cage is long enough for the rabbit? How can you test the cage?	The pet shop keeper needs to make a cage for the rabbit. Can you help by making one long enough and wide enough for the rabbit? How long do you think it will have to be? If more cages need to be made, can you find out exactly how long and how wide they should be? What could you use to measure with? Why is this a good choice?	Can you help the pet shop keeper to make a cage big enough for the rabbit? Estimate how long and how wide it will need to be? Measure your cage when you have built it. Was your estimate accurate?
Key vocabulary	• longer than • shorter than • narrower • thicker • wider • too short • too long • not long enough	• longer than • shorter than • narrower • wider • too short • not long enough • is as long as • is as wide as	• estimate • longer than • shorter than • centimetres long • centimetres wide
Opportunities for assessment	• can use mathematical vocabulary of length to explain activity • can compare two lengths • can explain how to test the size of the cage	• can compare two lengths • can make a sensible estimate • can select suitable non-standard units • can use selected units accurately	• can make a sensible estimate • can measure to the nearest centimetre using a ruler

Links with Y3 Activity

Research a small pet, its needs and size. Use the information to estimate how big its cage needs to be. Draw it accurately to scale.

ELG and PNS linked objectives

• FS: Use everyday language to talk about size and to compare objects (ELG)
• Y1: Estimate, measure and compare objects, choosing and using suitable uniform non-standard units (PNS)
• Y2: Estimate, compare and measure lengths, choosing and using standard units (PNS)
• Y3: Know the relationship between metres and centimetres and choose appropriate units to estimate, measure and record results (PNS)

Example 7.5   Snake-making game

Learning context: malleable materials

Learning objective: using vocabulary and units related to time.

	FS	Y1	Y2
Activity	Children explore dough and model snakes. They compare with others and count how many they have made during one minute, as measured by the sand timer.	As FS.	As FS.
Resources	Modelling dough; one-minute sand timer.	As FS.	In addition to FS: a written label asking 'How many snakes can you make in 1 minute?'
Prompt and key questions	How many snakes do you think you can make in 1 minute? Find out how many you can make before the sand runs out. Who has made the most? Do you make the same number each time?	How many snakes do you think you might make in 1 minute? Did you make the same number of snakes each time? How many do you think you might make in 2 minutes?	As Y1.
Key vocabulary	• before • while • after • next • minute	• before • after • during • minute	• before • after • during • minute
Opportunities for assessment	• can use vocabulary of time appropriately • demonstrates an understanding of when the activity begins and ends	• can use vocabulary of time appropriately • can use sand timer appropriately • shows an understanding of two minutes being twice as long	• can use vocabulary of time appropriately • can use sand timer appropriately • shows an understanding of two minutes being twice as long

Links with Y3 Activity
Record how many snakes you have made at five equal intervals. Record your start time. If your activity takes 10 minutes how long will the time interval be between each count?

ELG and PNS linked objectives
- FS: Use everyday language to talk about time (ELG)
- Y1: Use vocabulary related to time (PNS)
- Y2: Use units of time and know the relationships between them (PNS)
- Y3: Read the time on a 12 hour digital clock and calculate time intervals (PNS)

Example 7.6 Appointments at the vets

Learning context: role play

Learning objectives: using everyday language related to time and order familiar events

	FS	Y1	Y2
Activity	Children engage in vet surgery role play, using resources to write appointment cards, write opening and closing times, call patients and keep appointment book.	As FS.	As FS.
Resources	Soft toy animals; bandages; stethoscope; telephone; till; money; calendar; analogue clock; appointment cards; appointment book; opening and closing time sign; dressing up clothes; writing materials.	As FS.	As FS.
Prompt and key questions	The pet owners need to know what day and time to bring their pet again. The vet needs to know which animal to see first. Who is next? Who went before? How long will the bandage need to stay on for? When is your next appointment?	As FS.	The pet owners need to know when to bring their pets to the surgery. Can you write some appointment cards? What day and at what time will the animal have to come? Is that later or earlier than the last appointment?
Key vocabulary	• later • tomorrow • yesterday • days of the week • months • before • next • afterwards • weekend • morning • afternoon • evening	• days of the week • month names • weekend • morning • afternoon • evening • yesterday • tomorrow • minutes • hour • o'clock times	• days of the week • month names • weekend • fortnight • yesterday • tomorrow • minutes • hour • half an hour • quarter of an hour • o'clock times
Opportunities for assessment	• can sequence events in role play • uses vocabulary of time	• can sequence events in role play • uses vocabulary of time with increasing competence	• uses vocabulary of time with increasing competence • can read and write o'clock and half past times

Links with Y3 Activity

The vets start work at 9 a.m. They have lunch between 1 p.m. and 2 p.m. and finish work at 6 p.m. Appointments are every 20 minutes. Write out the appointment schedule for the day.

ELG and PNS linked objectives

• FS: Use everyday language to talk about time (ELG) order and sequence familiar events (PNS)
• Y1: Use vocabulary related to time to order days of the week (PNS)
• Y2: Use units of time and know the relationships between them (PNS)
• Y3: Read the time on a 12 hour digital clock to the nearest 5 minutes (PNS)

Planning, organizing and assessing independent play

This chapter covers:

- planning for playful mathematics teaching and independent play
- adult involvement in play
- assessing, recording and reporting
- photocopiable material to help with planning and assessment.

Planning

While guidance for mathematics planning is given in detail in a variety of documents and websites (see Resources), this chapter focuses on planning mathematics teaching with meaningful connection making in mind, and for independent play. As with all effective planning, practitioners need to assess where children are in terms of their own mathematical development, determined by observation and formative assessment, and where they need to go next. The planning of 'where next' can be set in playful and meaningful contexts by considering what the children's current interests are, or establishing a unifying learning theme.

Planning for a playful and meaningful context for mathematics teaching

Observing what motivates children, what they become involved in and what captures their imagination, informs practitioners of a suitable creative context in which to set their mathematics teaching. Figure 8.1 on p.110 illustrates some questions that practitioners might explore to help realize the mathematical potential of a variety of activities and how they can make links with other areas of learning. If these links with other learning areas are established, children are more able to make connections and make sense of their learning.

Planning for independent play

Once a creative context or theme has been decided on, then planning for continuous provision and independent play can begin.

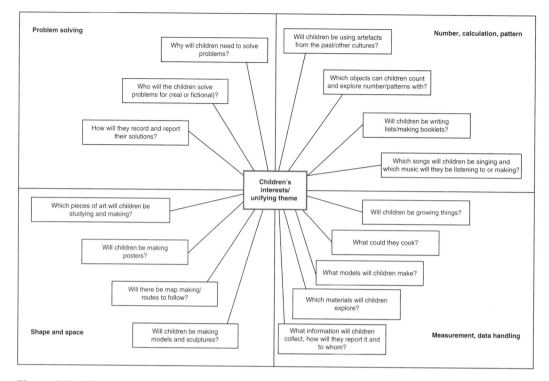

Figure 8.1   Planning a creative context for mathematics teaching

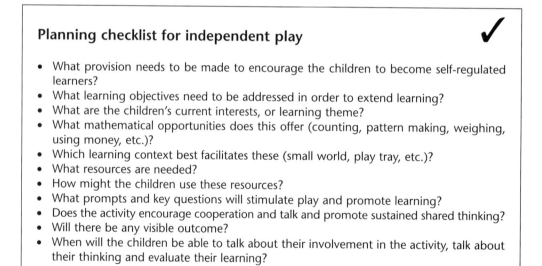

Planning for independent play should be recorded in ways that are helpful to the practitioner and reflect their intended learning outcomes. Figures 8.2 and 8.3 are examples of planning for play and independent activity for the Foundation Stage (birth to 5 years) and Key Stage 1 (5–7 years) (see Photocopiables 1 and 2 in the Appendices). The plans are:

- intended for a three-week period
- linked to areas of learning and development in the Foundation Stage and show links to areas of learning in Key Stage 1
- based on the theme of 'the sea'.

The practitioner cannot, of course, plan for child-initiated activity, as this will happen spontaneously, but the aim is to provide resources that motivate this. These activities and learning intentions can then be 'advertised' to the children, as seen in Figure 8.4. As the plans are thematic in nature, and show links between several learning areas, the practitioner can identify and highlight specific mathematical activity for inclusion in weekly planning or individual session plans (see Tables 8.2–8.4).

Planning for playful mathematics sessions

As previously discussed, child-initiated play and independent mathematical activity alone do not provide the systematic repeated experience and practice needed to ensure progression. Focused teaching groups must also be playful and meaningful; the adults should be actively teaching and subject-secure so that they can plan for progression (DCSF, 2008; Gifford, 2008; Siraj-Blatchford et al., 2002). As we have seen in Chapter 1, mathematics teaching and learning can be provided for by the mix of focused teaching and independent play. Tables 8.1–8.4 are exemplars of differentiated mathematics session plans for Reception (4–5 years) to Year 2 (6–7 years). Table 8.1 is an exemplar of a short session that can be used in conjunction with any of the exemplars. Tables 8.2–8.4 are exemplars of session plans that show focused teaching alongside independent play and which:

- provide ideas for resources in the playful context of 'the sea'
- act as a guide to illustrate how a session might be adapted and extended from Reception to Year 2
- follow the session structure illustrated in Figure 1.2
- make reference to ELGs and PNS linked objectives.

Organizing play

As seen in Chapter 2, the learning environment plays an important role in promoting good quality teaching and learning, both in its content and organization. While Chapter 1 considered a possible structure for teaching mathematics through play for a mixed-age class, its management will be considered here. In terms of the day-to-day running of a busy classroom, the children need to know which of the learning contexts in the continuous provision are available to them, what they might 'do' in these contexts (the practitioners' intended learning outcomes) and the expectations of how they are to be used, including transition from one context to the next. These learning contexts and associated learning intentions, or prompts, therefore need to be made known to the children, while the number of children visiting each context should be monitored to avoid crushes in one particular area. This can be achieved in a variety of ways:

- A 'play board' or 'play menu' can be used (see Figure 8.4 on p.123–4). Here, drawings or photographs of the learning contexts are posted alongside the practitioner's written prompt with questions to stimulate play. Once they have been explained to the children, they act as a visual reminder. Some practitioners encourage the children to indicate which contexts they have visited, by writing their name beside each picture or attaching a named peg. This also acts as a means of recording which learning contexts the child has visited during the day or week.

Role play

- **Learning opportunities and curriculum links**

  Ice-cream kiosk

  Developing related narrative, writing price lists/shop signs (Lit); counting/sorting spoons, ice-cream tubs and cones, etc.; writing prices on items to sell; reading numerals on price lists/telephone and telephone book; using coins to make values and give change (Maths); using maps to give directions (UW/geography)

- **Resources**

  Writing materials; till; coins; telephone and telephone directory; calendar; clock; bags and purses; assorted ice-cream tubs/cartons; paper cones; assorted spoons and ice-cream scoop; maps and postcards; dressing-up clothes

Small-world drama

- **Learning opportunities and curriculum links**

  Journey to the seaside

  Developing narrative (CL/lit); designing and making train layout, using positional/geographical language (Maths, UW/maths, geography); counting/sorting/making patterns with vehicles and farm animals (Maths)

  The Bear's Adventure

  Developing own narrative and retelling story (CL/lit); counting/sorting/making patterns with shells/farm animals (Maths/lit); using positional and geographical language (Maths, UW, EAD/lit, geography)

- **Resources**

  Train track; farm animals; fencing; vehicles; play people; shells; pebbles; driftwood; teddy; sea animals; boats; buildings

Table-top activity

- **Learning opportunities and curriculum links**

  Marble run of chosen number; counting/ordering/matching to numeral 0–10 staircase using acorns, shells, doublooms; making chosen number using Numicon® (Maths); marble run using Numicon® (Maths); marble run chosen letter; letter-matching games (Lit)

- **Resources**

  Marble runs; acorns; shells; number lines 0–10; Numicon®

Reading and listening activity

- **Learning opportunities and curriculum links**

  Reading big sentence maker; reading in book corner a selection of self-chosen books; reading book of the week; reading labels and signs in the environment; listening to a selection of story tapes and rhymes (CL/lit)

- **Resources**

  Selected book; story tapes

Figure 8.2 Independent play

(Continued)

Figure 8.2 (Continued)

	Learning opportunities and curriculum links		Learning opportunities and curriculum links
 Creative and aesthetic	**Learning opportunities and curriculum links** Modelling and painting chosen letter (Lit, PD, EAD/lit); modelling and painting chosen numeral (Maths, PD, EAD/maths); modelling/counting/sorting/sharing and grouping dough shells and treasure (PD/maths); painting characters in selected book (EAD, Lit/maths, art); painting historical seaside artefacts (EAD, UW/art, history) **Resources** Modelling dough; paint; book of the week; historical resources	 *Graphics area*	**Learning opportunities and curriculum links** Making booklets about chosen letter/word/book; writing lists and postcards (Lit); making booklets about chosen number/shapes/things longer and shorter than; filling in empty number lines; ordering numerals (Maths); drawing and making maps for pirates (CL, UW/lit, geography) **Resources** Paper; staples; scissors; glue sticks; writing materials; numbered and empty number lines; sheets of numerals 0–20; rulers
 ICT	**Learning opportunities and curriculum links** Using a selection of simple computer programs to create signs/price lists for ice-cream kiosk (UW, maths, EAD/ICT) **Resources** 2Simple paint program	 *Washing line*	**Learning opportunities and curriculum links** Ordering numeral cards; finding a missing numeral in a sequence; making patterns with sea-related pictures (Maths); ordering historical postcards (UW/history) **Resources** Numeral cards 0–10/0–20; sea postcards; pictures of seaside artefacts; old postcards of holidays in the past

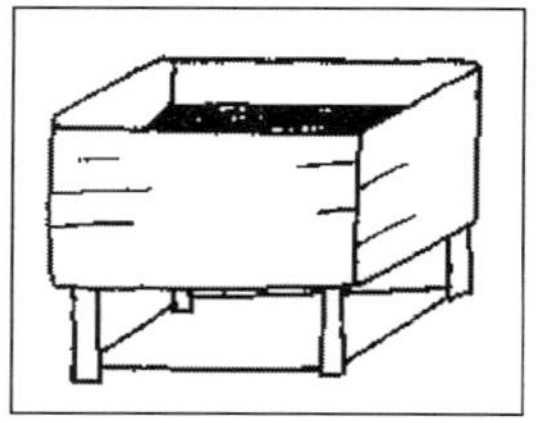

Play tray 1

- **Learning opportunities and curriculum links**

  Sea creatures
  Retelling story of Bear's Adventure and developing own narrative with sea creatures/artefacts; counting/sorting/matching sea creatures/boats (CL, EAD/lit)

  Pirate's grog
  Pouring and filling tankards with coloured water; estimating and measuring capacities of a selection of tankards (Maths); developing pirate role play (CL, EAD/lit)

- **Resources**
  Blue-coloured water; assorted sea animals; assorted boats; small teddy; pebbles; driftwood; small plastic box (treasure chest); assorted tankards; plastic flagon

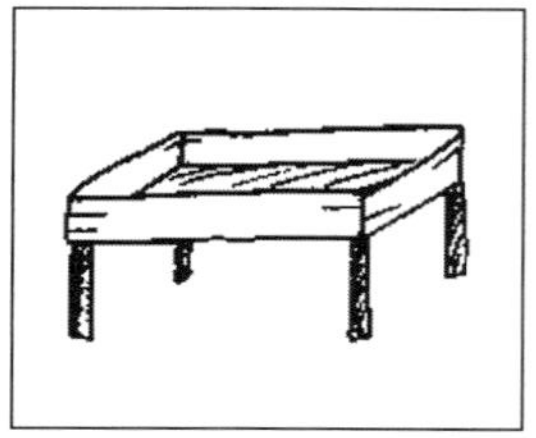

Play tray 2

- **Learning opportunities and curriculum links**

  Mirrors
  Using mirrors and half pictures of boats to explore reflection and symmetry (Maths, UW/maths, science)

  Coloured telescopes
  Using cardboard telescopes and coloured transparent paper to view through and discuss how colours change (UW/science)

- **Resources**
  Pairs of toy sea creatures; half pictures of boats on card; mirrors; cardboard cylinders; sticky tape; transparent gel

Construction

- **Learning opportunities and curriculum links**

  Duplo®
  Designing a train layout for a journey to the beach and using positional language

  Wooden blocks
  Making buildings in a seaside town

  Lasy®
  Making a bus to transport play people to a seaside town (UW, PD, maths/technology, maths)

- **Resources**
  Duplo®; wooden bricks; Lasy®

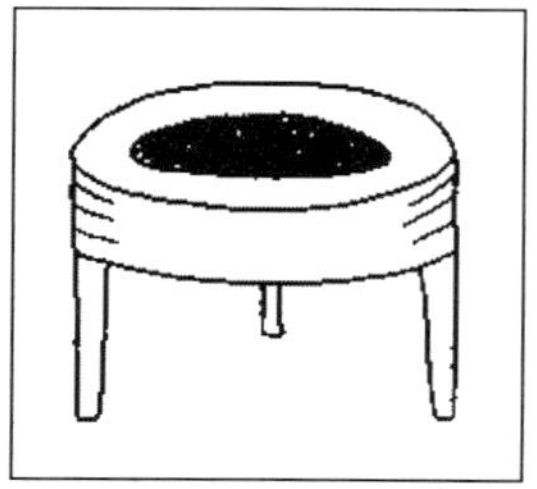

Play tray 3

- **Learning opportunities and curriculum links**

  Sea rubbish
  Exploring a selection of beach 'rubbish' with magnets, sorting items that are/are not magnetic (UW, Maths, CL/science)

  Telescopes and binoculars
  Making telescopes and binoculars for pirates using cutting and joining skills (PD, UW, maths/technology)

- **Resources**
  A selection of magnetic/non-magnetic items and packaging; cardboard cylinders; sticky tape; scissors; pens

Figure 8.2 Independent play

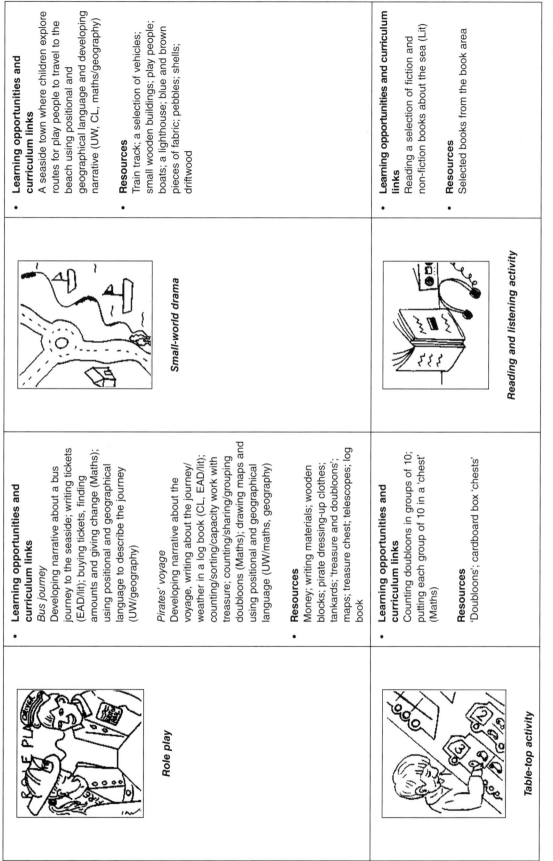

Role play • **Learning opportunities and curriculum links** *Bus journey* Developing narrative about a bus journey to the seaside; writing tickets (EAD/lit); buying tickets, finding amounts and giving change (Maths); using positional and geographical language to describe the journey (UW/geography) *Pirates' voyage* Developing narrative about the voyage, writing about the journey/ weather in a log book (CL, EAD/lit); counting/sorting/capacity work with treasure; counting/sharing/grouping doubloons (Maths); drawing maps and using positional and geographical language (UW/maths, geography) • **Resources** Money; writing materials; wooden blocks; pirate dressing-up clothes; tankards; 'treasure and doubloons'; maps; treasure chest; telescopes; log book	**Small-world drama** • **Learning opportunities and curriculum links** A seaside town where children explore routes for play people to travel to the beach using positional and geographical language and developing narrative (UW, CL, maths/geography) • **Resources** Train track; a selection of vehicles; small wooden buildings; play people; boats; a lighthouse; blue and brown pieces of fabric; pebbles; shells; driftwood
Table-top activity • **Learning opportunities and curriculum links** Counting doubloons in groups of 10; putting each group of 10 in a 'chest' (Maths) • **Resources** 'Doubloons'; cardboard box 'chests'	**Reading and listening activity** • **Learning opportunities and curriculum links** Reading a selection of fiction and non-fiction books about the sea (Lit) • **Resources** Selected books from the book area

Figure 8.3 Independent play in the outdoor teaching and learning area

(Continued)

Figure 8.3 (Continued)

 Creative and aesthetic area	• **Learning opportunities and curriculum links** Painting chosen letter/word; painting characters from the book of the week (Lit); painting chosen number (Maths); painting in response to Andy Goldsworthy's work (EAD/art) • **Resources** Paint; paper; card	
 Graphics area		• **Learning opportunities and curriculum links** Writing road signs for bus journey role play, bus tickets and signs; writing letters to pirates and in log books (Lit); drawing maps (UW/geography); writing the number of the week; writing price lists for bus tickets (Maths) • **Resources** Pens; card; scissors; sheets of photocopied numerals 0–20; numbers in sand and empty number lines
 Garden	• **Learning opportunities and curriculum links** Selecting a watering can to fill and water hyacinths (UW, maths/science, maths) • **Resources** Graduated watering cans	
 Sandpit		• **Learning opportunities and curriculum links** Making the letter/word of the week and driving a car/truck around shape made (CL/lit); making chosen number and driving a car/truck around shape (Maths); pouring/filling; exploring capacity; estimating and measuring (Maths) • **Resources** A selection of buckets and containers; rakes; small cars and trucks

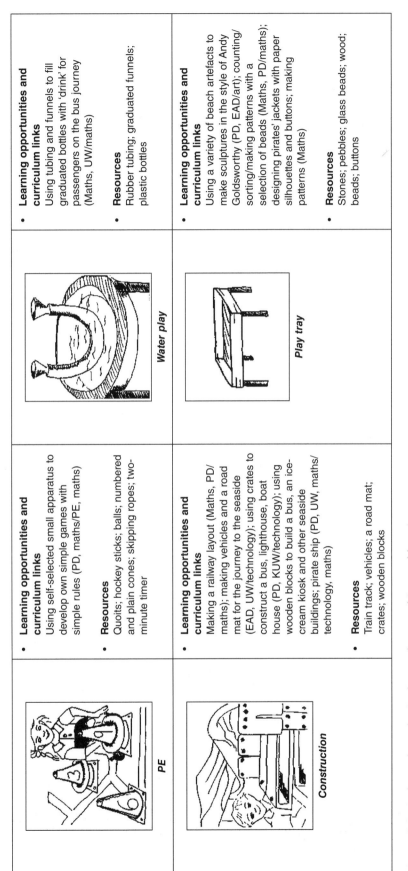

	Learning opportunities and curriculum links
PE	Using self-selected small apparatus to develop own simple games with simple rules (PD, maths/PE, maths) • **Resources** Quoits; hockey sticks; balls; numbered and plain cones; skipping ropes; two-minute timer
Water play	Using tubing and funnels to fill graduated bottles with 'drink' for passengers on the bus journey (Maths, UW/maths) • **Resources** Rubber tubing; graduated funnels; plastic bottles
Construction	Making a railway layout (Maths, PD/maths); making vehicles and a road mat for the journey to the seaside (EAD, UW/technology); using crates to construct a bus, lighthouse, boat house (PD, KUW/technology); using wooden blocks to build a bus, an ice-cream kiosk and other seaside buildings; pirate ship (PD, UW, maths/technology, maths) • **Resources** Train track; vehicles; a road mat; crates; wooden blocks
Play tray	Using a variety of beach artefacts to make sculptures in the style of Andy Goldsworthy (PD, EAD/art); counting/sorting/making patterns with a selection of beads (Maths, PD/maths); designing pirates' jackets with paper silhouettes and buttons; making patterns (Maths) • **Resources** Stones; pebbles; glass beads; wood; beads; buttons

Figure 8.3 Independent play in the outdoor teaching and learning area

Table 8.1 Mental/oral calculation

Learning objectives: counting in steps of 10.

Key vocabulary: counting on/counting back; more/greater than; less/smaller than; 10s and 1s; partition.
Resources: counting stick; small-world fish; digit flip books 0–100/whiteboards/pens.

Direct teaching

Indicate the 0 and 100 end of the counting stick and explain that the fish is going to swim along its length, 'resting' at the marks which represent a 10s number. Children count in 10s from 0 to 100 and back. Rest the fish in the middle of the stick. Ask the children to indicate on flip books or whiteboards which number the fish is resting on and to discuss and explain how they know it must be 50. Rest the fish at other intervals along the stick and ask the children to indicate which number it represents and to explain their thinking.

Extension: Ask the children to indicate the number which is 10 more or less than the number where the fish rests. Ask them to indicate the number that is its partner to make 100, then count on to check. Rest the fish in between two marks and ask the children to calculate what number its position represents. Ask them to discuss their reasoning and to partition their answer into 10s and 1s.

ELG and PNS linked objectives

- FS: Count aloud in 1s and 10s (PNS)
- Y1: Count on or back in 1s and 10s and use this knowledge to derive multiples of 10 (PNS)
- Y2: Count in 10s and explain what each digit represents in a two-digit number and derive and recall all addition and subtraction facts for all pairs of multiples of 10 with totals up to 100 (PNS)

Table 8.2 Session focus: addition and subtraction

Learning objective: solving problems involving addition.

Key vocabulary: counting on/counting back; more/greater than; less/smaller than; adding; subtracting; take away; equals; the same as.

Resources: 10 small-world fishes; small nets; large blue cloth (the 'sea'); large floor number line 0 to 10; individual number lines 0 to 10; Numicon®; whiteboards and pens.

Introduction and direct teaching	Focused teaching/Guided group work	Independent work
Make explicit the learning objectives and key vocabulary in the context of a fisherman making 2 catches of fish. Explain that the task is to find out how many fish the fisherman catches, and to keep a 'record'. Using the nets, make 2 catches, ensuring that the numbers in each are different. How many fish are there altogether? Repeat with different numbers, making reference to the number line. Model the correct algorithms as a 'record'.	Ask each child in turn to make 2 catches and combine the 2 groups to determine how many altogether. Relate this to a large floor number line as before. Repeat using different numbers, reinforcing that 2 groups can be combined in any order. Introduce the idea of fish escaping to illustrate subtraction as 'take away' and relate to the floor number line by jumping back.	Play tray: Can you make a record of the fish you catch with the nets? Modelling materials: Make 2 groups of sea creatures. Can you record how many you have altogether? Graphics area: Can you make a poster advertising the best 2 catches of the day. How many fish are there?
Extension: Relate this to the floor number line by asking a child to relate the addition of 2 groups to jumps along the floor number line. Explore the outcome if the catches are added in a different order, again relating to the number line.	Extension: Explain that 4 fish and 3 fish are caught making a total of 7. Then 3 fish escape. Use jumps forward and back along the number line and the groups of fish and overlay the corresponding Numicon® plates to demonstrate images and connections between the inverse relationship.	Table-top: Take 2 pieces of Numicon® from the bag (0–10) and use them to help record a fish addition and subtraction story.

Introduce independent play activities and direct groups.

Review time and plenary: Ask a group of children to discuss and review their independent work.
Probing question: Can you show and talk about the connection between addition and subtraction using 2 groups of fish?

ELG and PNS linked objectives

- FS: Using quantities and objects, children add and subtract two single-digit numbers and count on or back to find the answer (ELG)
- Y1: Relate addition to counting on and recognize that addition can be done in any order (PNS)
- Y2: Understand that subtraction is the inverse of addition and vice versa (PNS)

Table 8.3 Session focus: estimating, counting and place value

Learning objectives:

- Estimating numbers and checking by counting.
- Beginning to use knowledge of place value to order numbers.

Key vocabulary: estimate; guess; more than/less than; 10s and 1s; partition; more than/greater than; in between.
Resources: *The Lighthouse Keeper's Lunch* (see Resources); IWB; 100 'breadsticks' (short lengths of art straws, or similar); 10 bundles of 10 'breadsticks'; 10 paper plates; dice; number lines, both numbered and empty; whiteboards and pens.

Introduction and direct teaching	Focused teaching/Guided group work	Independent work
Remind the children about the story of the Grinlings and how Mrs Grinling prepares lunch for Mr Grinling. Make explicit the learning objectives and key vocabulary in the context of Mrs Grinling putting breadsticks in bundles of 10. Use the IWB with images of breadsticks and ask the children to estimate how many breadsticks they can see. What would be a quick way to count them? Ask a child to count and collect 10 breadsticks together. Count the resultant 'bundles' in 10s.	Give each child a handful of 'breadsticks'. Ask them to estimate how many they have and to compare their estimates with others. Ask them to check their estimate by counting. Was it more or less than their estimate? Ask them to find the number on the number line. Was anyone's estimate accurate? Whose was the closest?	Play tray: How many fishes do you think there are? Can you put fishes in bags of 10? Can you count in 10s how many there are?
		Modelling materials: Can you make 10 pieces of food for Mr Grinling?
	Extension: Mrs Grinling introduces a game to make it fun to pack the breadsticks. Each child rolls a dice, collects the corresponding number of breadsticks and records the number. When 10 breadsticks are gathered, they are exchanged for a bundle of 10. Reinforce that 21, for example, is 2 bundles of 10 and a 1. Discuss how this is written and what each digit represents. At the end of the game, children count their total number in 10s, write the number and position it on the empty number line representing 0 to 100. Ask them to discuss their reasoning and to partition their number into 10s and 1s.	Washing line: Can you hang these numbers (random numbers from 0 to 100) on the 'pulley' in the right order?
Introduce independent activities and direct groups.		Role play: Mrs Grinling would like to set the table with 10 pieces of food on each plate.
		Table-top: Take a handful of shells, estimate how many you have and then count accurately. Write the number and place it where you think it is on an empty number line.

Review time and plenary: Ask a group of children to discuss and review their independent work. Count 23 breadsticks, for example, in bundles of 10s and 1s. Probing question: Can you partition into 10s and 1s and say which digit is worth more – the 3 or the 2?

ELG and PNS linked objectives

- FS: Count reliably with numbers from 1 to 20 (ELG). Estimate how many objects they can see and check by counting (PNS FS)
- Y1: Use knowledge of place value to position numbers, 0–20, on a number line (PNS)
- Y2: Count up to 100 objects by grouping in 10s and explain what each digit in a two-digit number represents (PNS)

Table 8.4 Session focus: space, position and turns

Learning objective: using mathematical vocabulary to describe whole, half and quarter turns.

Key vocabulary: forwards; backwards; sideways; left; right; whole, half, quarter turns; clockwise; anti-clockwise.

Resources: programmable toy; large sheet of thick blue paper (the 'sea') with grid drawn on (each square the same length as the programmable toy); small-world boats/lighthouses/sea creatures, etc; a large paper circle, semi-circle and quarter circle; vocabulary cards for key vocabulary (above); captain's hat (or similar).

Introduction and direct teaching	Focused teaching/Guided group work	Independent work
Make explicit the learning objectives in the context of a boat lost at sea that needs directions. Place small-world objects around the floor and ask a child to be the captain. Modelling key vocabulary, give the child directions to cross the floor, avoiding the obstacles.	Ask children around 'the sea' grid to position the small-world objects. Encourage them to describe where they are placing the objects in relation to other objects and children. Put a play person on top of a programmable toy; this is the captain on the lost boat. Using the grid, ask the children to estimate how far they need to send the boat from one object to the next. Encourage them to use key vocabulary to describe their route, and then program the toy to follow it.	Small-world drama: make up a story about the lost boat. What does it find on its journey? Draw and describe to a friend a picture map of the scene for the logbook.
Extension: introduce whole, half and quarter turns, using clockwise and anti-clockwise vocabulary. Lay chosen paper shape on the floor to act as a 'turn silhouette' for the child to move around to encourage understanding of whole, half and quarter.		Role play: give directions to the captain (development of 'instant' role play from direct teaching scenario).
Introduce independent work and direct groups.	Extension: using the vocabulary cards to ensure key vocabulary is used, children work in pairs. One child gives directions, while the other programs the toy accordingly.	Graphics area: draw a map/write directions to tell the boat how to get out of the fog. Tell a friend.

Table-top: use the 2D shapes to make a picture of the missing boat and the scene. |

Review time and plenary: Ask a group of children to discuss and review their independent work. Encourage the children to use key vocabulary when describing resultant maps or written directions.

ELG and PNS linked objectives

- FS: Use everyday words to describe position (ELG)
- Y1: Recognize and make whole, half and quarter turns (PNS)
- Y2: Recognize and make whole, half and quarter turns, both clockwise and anti-clockwise (PNS)

- Can you use the Lasy to make a bus big enough to carry **5** people to the seaside?
- Can you make a bus big enough to carry double the number of passengers?

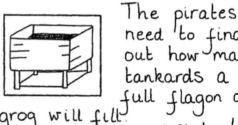

The pirates need to find out how many tankards a full flagon of grog will fill.
- Can you help and find out how many?
- Can you find a way of recording your results?

- How do the sea pictures change when you hold a mirror against them?
- Can you make your own symmetrical sea picture? Fold it in half and use a mirror!

- Can you help sort the beach rubbish for recycling?
- How many things are magnetic?
- Can you find a way to record which things are magnetic and which are not?

- Can you make some price tags for things in the kiosk?
- You have 20p to spend in the kiosk What will you buy?

On the train to the seaside the passengers notice the farm animals are in a pattern
- Can you put the animals in a pattern?
- What sort of pattern is it?

- Can you paint **5** pirates?
- The pirate finds **5** pieces of treasure Can you use the dough to make them? Can you make double the number?

- Can you use the shells to make a number staircase? What do you notice?
- Can you use the things on the table to find different ways of making **5**?

- Today there are **5** fishes in the net
- What do you know about **5**? Can you make a book about **5**?
- Can you show **5** on a number line?

Figure 8.4   Independent play menu

- Sashes, badges or posters can be used to inform children about how many of them can use a particular context at any one time. If it is practical to have a maximum of four children at a particular play tray, for example, then four sashes or clip-on badges might be made available for the children to put on when they visit this area. Once the sashes are all being used, the context is 'full'. Similarly, posters at each context can remind the children of suitable participant numbers, the most successful of which show the numeral, the written word and an array of the number.

Adult involvement

As seen in Chapter 2, adult intervention through the use of prompts and questioning is most effective when done appropriately and sensitively. Adults, whether professionals or parent helpers, can be involved in play in a variety of ways:

- Visiting adults and parent helpers can be effective in helping to extend and support mathematical development once they understand the nature of the play the child is engaged in, and the learning intentions the practitioner has planned for each learning context. Attaching the written prompt and key questions beside each learning context not only helps to reinforce this for the children, but also acts as a means of communicating to adults the nature of the intended activity. When starting statutory schooling, children may lack the requisite skills to select and use learning contexts appropriately; by having written intentions immediately available for adults to see, they can help to support the youngest children as they learn the routines of the environment.
- Practitioners should plan opportunities where they are available to talk to children about their involvement in play and ask open questions, thus addressing a balance of practitioner and child agendas. This in turn will aid assessment.
- Adults can take digital photographs or films of play. Once again, this shows the children that adults are both interested in and value what they are doing. These can act as records of the activity for displays and portfolios.

Assessing, recording and reporting

Opportunities for assessing independent play will arise when:

- target observations are made of a specific child, group of children or a learning context during play
- there is sustained shared thinking
- children report back at review time or as part of a plenary.

During these situations, practitioners can note:

- whether children are interacting and talking with others
- the children's engagement, motivation and thinking
- the mathematical vocabulary children are using
- how children are using resources

- whether children are involved in practitioner-initiated, practitioner-initiated–child-continued or self-initiated play
- which learning outcomes have been addressed.

Recorded observations of play can be matched to assessment criteria to show the practitioner 'where the child is' and 'where the child needs to go next', thus informing planning. They can take the form of:

- brief observations and annotated photos
- notes made on a pro forma (see Photocopiable 3 in the Appendices), which constitutes part of a child's ongoing assessments, aspects of which can be used to inform recording in the Early Years Foundation Stage Profile.

Assessments will also be made during review time where four to six children in a large class can report back on their independent play. This allows the practitioner to assess the child's involvement in the activity, along with the success of the planned continuous provision. Figure 8.5 is an example of recorded assessments made during this time. A blank version of this sheet has been provided for your own use (see Photocopiable 4). Practitioners will need to report children's progress to parents and this is considered in Chapter 9.

Date	Name	Activity undertaken (practitioner- or child-initiated?)	Comments on learning (learning dispositions and objectives addressed)
5/10	Shinaz	Practitioner-initiated–child-continued. Worked in the graphics area to make a number line from 0 to 14. Drew circles around even numbers 2–12. Coloured number line and stapled to make a bracelet.	Motivated by the activity and used own ideas to join the number line and make into a 'number line bracelet'. Shows awareness of even numbers.
5/10	Kaleb	Child-initiated. Used Numicon® plates to press into clay.	Motivated to explore mark making with Numicon®. Used own ideas to collect and use Numicon®. Was able to talk about the prints he made and could count up to six marks accurately.

Figure 8.5 Record and assessment sheet for review time

Children's self-assessment

Providing opportunities for children to be involved in self-assessment gives the practitioner a greater understanding of the child, and allows the child to see themselves as a self-regulated learner who has ownership of their discoveries and ideas. Using prompts and open questions, the child can be encouraged to verbalize their thinking and practice using language for learning (see Chapter 1). Starting points for reflective discussion and self-assessment include:

- looking through the child's portfolio, learning journey or story
- looking together at annotated photos of mathematical activity
- a review time when the child reports back on independent play.

Creative ideas for good practice

- Select a motivating theme, based on children's interests in which to set mathematics (both in focused teaching sessions and in independent play), which allows good cross-curricular links to be made.
- Plan independent play and activity carefully, identifying learning objectives or outcomes, an appropriate learning context to facilitate these, suitable resources and imaginative ways for children to record outcomes (if appropriate).
- Ensure children know which learning contexts are available to them, how they are to be used and the planned learning intentions.
- Involve adults in supporting children in their play by planning time for them to observe children at play, and to make sensitive interactions.
- Allow children time to report back about their play, to share what they have discovered and links they have made in their learning.
- Value adult-initiated play and child-initiated play equally, ensuring that children have opportunities to report back on both.
- Make assessments of children's mathematical development through observations of their play, interactions with them, and during their reporting back.

Glossary

CL: communication and literacy.

EAD: expressive arts and design.

PD: physical development.

PSED: personal, social and emotional development.

UW: understanding the world.

Further reading

Carr, M. and Lee, W. (2012) *Learning Stories: Constructing Learner Identities in Early Education*. London: Sage Publications. Based on their work in New Zealand, the authors explore theory and case studies exemplifying learning stories as a means of demonstrating children's learning dispositions and involvement of families.

Hutchin, V. (2012) *Assessing and Supporting Young Children's Learning for the Early Years Foundation Stage*. London: Hodder Education. This text gives practical suggestions for observation and collecting information for making judgements in the EYFS.

Podmore, V.N. and Luff, P. (2012) *Observations: Origins and Approaches*. Maidenhead: Open University Press/McGraw-Hill. This is a comprehensive book detailing theory underpinning the practice of observation and techniques of observation for research and day-to-day practice.

9

Parents as partners: involving parents in mathematics and play

This chapter covers:

- a brief discussion of the role of parental involvement as described in recent legislation
- the benefits of involving parents in their child's mathematical education
- family learning programmes
- strategies for involving parents in their child's early years mathematics education.

Why work with parents?

If children are to perceive themselves as capable mathematicians, then they need to feel confident and positive about themselves as learners and doers of mathematics. Involving parents in their child's mathematics education plays a significant part in how a child feels about and engages with the subject. There is increasing awareness that a child's early experiences have lasting influence on their development and attitude of themselves as learners (DfE, 2011). A review by Frank Field MP (Field, 2010) emphasizes the importance of improving parenting skills and supporting children's early development as a means of ending the inter-generational transmission of child poverty and improving life chances. Differences in parental involvement have a greater impact on a child's achievement than differences associated with variations in the quality of schooling at primary age: what parents do with their children at home has far greater significance than any other factor open to educational influence (Desforges, 2003). Problems associated with parental involvement, however, often arise because many parents are influenced by their own experience of mathematics education and find it difficult to re-engage with the process. While parents who are confident with maths and eager to help their child will have a positive impact on the child as a learner, it follows that parents who have not enjoyed a good relationship with the subject, and who feel 'no good' at maths, may have a negative impact on their child's learning. In this case, it seems likely that the child will grow to believe maths is 'hard and boring'; there is a clear link between parents with low-level mathematical skills and their children's underachievement in mathematics (DCSF, 2008). Without positive intervention, therefore, it is all too easy to see how a cycle of underachievement in mathematics might be perpetuated. The key, then, to empowering children to view themselves as mathematicians is for practitioners and teachers to provide opportunities for parents to reassess their relationship with mathematics. If parents can begin to realize that mathematics can be creative, exciting and fun, they may then believe attainment in the subject is desirable and achievable.

It is, in fact, their child's level of attainment in mathematics that strongly influences the level of parental involvement. If a parent is given the opportunity to see their child as 'being a mathematician' (see below), they are then more likely to want to become involved themselves (Desforges, 2003). There have been several projects whose aim has been to raise children's attainment in mathematics through parental involvement, notably the Ocean Maths Project (cited in DCSF, 2008). The success of this project, and others, has been to involve parents in workshops that aim to help adults enjoy maths activities and to change their attitudes to maths both at home, school and in the community. Young children often act as 'mathematical connection-makers', making links between the mathematical experiences they have had in the home and those they have at school. Such projects provide parents with a window into this 'connection-making' process, thus enabling them to support their child's mathematical development with greater understanding and confidence.

Promoting parents' involvement with their child's maths can:

- encourage them to have a more positive approach to the subject
- help bring parents up to date with current strategies and approaches
- provide parents with the shared language of mathematics
- enable parents to discover the cumulative nature of mathematics and its progression
- allow parents to see their child as a capable mathematician
- encourage a shared interest in the subject with their child.

Family learning programmes

At its most literal, these programmes bring family members together to work and learn collaboratively on a particular theme or focus and can be run by any interested and qualified persons or group. More specifically, family learning programs can be run by local authority registered family learning tutors. Many programmes aim to help parents learn how best to support their child's learning and often include elements of basic skills learning in maths or literacy, along with offering opportunities for parents to study for national tests, although this is not their main focus.

The Pen Green Centre in Corby has been revolutionary in terms of establishing a rigorous and well-respected programme of family involvement and community education. Its work with the community has led them to develop a specific pedagogy described as the Parents' Involvement in their Children's Learning (PICL) Programme (Whalley, 2007). This has resulted in staff from many early years settings receiving training to enable them to understand more fully how their work with parents can have not only a positive impact on the learning of the child, but also on the parents and on the community as a whole. This approach is based on four concepts:

- involvement
- well-being
- adult style
- schemas.

Time is devoted to giving parents opportunities to learn about these concepts to enable them to understand more fully how their child can learn. Through observations of, and discussions with, their own child, they build up a picture of their child as a powerful learner.

Case study: Two Moors Family Learning Group

Influenced by the Pen Green model of parental involvement, the Family Learning Group at Two Moors Primary School in Devon supports parents in observing their child's play, identifying schemas and building up a portfolio of their child's play and experiences.

During one particular programme, supported by external funding, the group chose the focus 'Mathematical development as observed in young children's play'. Over several weeks, parents of under-4s were encouraged to:

- find out about schemas through tuition with the family learning tutor
- observe and photograph their child play in nursery and engage in mathematical activities with their child
- observe their child's play at home and repeat activities observed and participated in at school
- attend a planned visit to a local forest, supported by tutors, to collect natural materials used to stimulate play and explore repeating patterns
- attend sessions led by the family learning tutor and an early years teacher to discover more about early years mathematics, the place of mathematics in the EYFS and its progression into Key Stage 1 (5–7 years)
- use information gathered to compile a portfolio about their child's schematic play, highlighting mathematical aspects.

Using their observations, photos and discussions with other members of the group, parents were able to identify their child's schemas and particular mathematical interests. With support from the tutor, they were able to compile portfolios that not only showed their child to be an active and independent learner, but also a competent and emerging mathematician. Parents involved in the programme felt they:

- could more clearly identify aspects of their child's mathematical development in day-to-day routines and play
- were more confident in their use of language to support mathematical development
- could provide play things which best suited their child's individual interests and learning
- had gained some understanding of how mathematics education starts in the early years and progresses into primary school.

Involving parents in playful mathematics

Most importantly, parents need to feel welcome. An atmosphere of friendliness, respect and trust must be established first; if a parent feels uncomfortable coming into a setting or classroom, they are unlikely to repeat the experience. Once parents feel welcome, they will be more receptive to initiatives showing them that mathematics is creative, exciting and to be enjoyed with their child. There are several strategies for involving parents in playful mathematics:

- Make sure that the environment is as light and attractive as possible and that a practitioner is free to talk to parents as they come into the setting or classroom.
- Give parents the opportunity to observe mathematics sessions, ensuring they see a mix of focused teaching and independent playful maths. This will allow them to see how mathematics can be interesting and creative and make connections with other areas of learning and the child's interests. It will also allow parents to become aware of progression as staff talk about the learning that preceded the observed session, and the teaching and learning that will follow. It may also give parents the opportunity to understand more about sustained shared thinking.
- Invite parents to regular story-time sessions during which stories that explore mathematical concepts are read (see Resources). This gives the practitioner the opportunity to model effective practice such as singing counting songs and rhymes, using number lines (see Chapter 4), clapping patterns and modelling a range of mathematical vocabulary.
- Lend out maths games, such as board games, pattern-making games, games with clocks.
- Involve parents in making maths story sacks, which will stimulate ideas. Local libraries and Children's Centres often have a good supply to lend out.
- Give parents booklets about aspects of mathematics illustrated with photos and examples of children's mathematical graphics.
- Encourage parents to look at displays of mathematical graphics and annotated photos of children engaged in playful mathematics. It is important to indicate whether the photos are of self-initiated or adult-led learning and exactly which mathematical skills the child is learning and practising.
- Hold maths 'story trails' (see below).
- Provide early work which is maths based. Encourage parents to be involved in a maths-based task when the children come into their classroom. Such a task might be to notice how the pattern of harvest fruit on display has changed from the previous day, to hang clothes on a small washing line in a repeating pattern, or to find and record 'hidden number bonds' in a 3D display.
- Encourage the use of a graphics board where children and parents can make mathematical marks collectively. Children and parents are invited to write a response to questions posted on the board such as, 'How many people live in your house?' and 'What is your favourite number?'

⠄⡷⠄ Creative ideas for good practice

As a means of encouraging parents to see maths as enjoyable and achievable and to provide a family-friendly way to model mathematical activities, invite parents to a maths story sack workshop:

- Choose a good children's story which offers lots of mathematical potential (see Resources).
- Identify mathematical activities and games suggested by the story such as pattern making, matching the number of objects to numerals, making number lines, making price tags, and so on.
- Invite parents to join the making workshop and have a sample story sack there for them to see.
- Introduce them to the book and discuss and model all of the mathematical opportunities suggested by the book. Not only does this enable parents to make their own suggestions, but allows them to see mathematical opportunities they otherwise might not have, and raise the mathematical profile of such activities as pattern making and the use of mathematical vocabulary.
- Identify which resources, relevant to the book, are going to be made and how.
- Provide a comfortable and welcoming room where parents can meet and work together over a series of weeks to develop the project.

⠄⡷⠄ Creative ideas for good practice

The mathematical potential of storybooks, and the meaningful connections between literacy and mathematics, can be highlighted by mathematical story trails:

- Choose a book with lots of opportunities for mathematical activities and read to the children and parents (see Resources).
- Take the children and parents on a trail around the school in which you have placed mathematical encounters related to the book. These might include spotting the repeating pattern of clothes hanging on a washing line, finding the longest and shortest broom or the heaviest and lightest sack of corn.
- Use each encounter to model effective practice.
- Take photos of the trail to annotate and display later to highlight the mathematical potential of the activities encountered.

Dialogue with parents about maths and play

A partnership between parents and teachers can only be established if parents feel their views are both invited and valued. There will be little of a partnership if liaison is based upon the teacher telling the parent 'how it's done'. Real dialogue can be achieved through the family learning opportunities described above, but not exclusively so. This dialogue can also be achieved in any setting or classroom where early years staff are keen to facilitate it. Parents can and should be involved in assessment of their young child's mathematical development. This can be achieved regularly through a variety of strategies:

- Using a 'working wall'. A 'working wall' or 'observation wall' is a large display board on which practitioners display a mix of dated written observations of the children, or annotated photos. The display acts as a means of celebrating skills and interests the children are currently showing. Parents are also encouraged to pin up observations they have made of their children, or annotated photos, showing significant achievements, such as the first time a child puts on their shoes and socks, or writes their name. This acts as a way of keeping both practitioners and parents regularly informed and, importantly, ensures that parents contribute to the observation, assessment and planning cycle. This will then inform the planning of continuous provision effectively based on children's achievements and interests. While some parents do not like their observations of their child being on display for all to see, they may be more comfortable posting them in an 'observation folder' attached to the wall.

- Making portfolios of children's progress in the Foundation Stage. Using portfolios or 'learning journey' books is also a successful way of involving parents. Displaying annotated photos and mathematical graphics in this way allows parents to see the child engaged in activities they might otherwise be unaware of. Including annotated photos of children engaged in playful mathematics acts to highlight the mathematical content of much of a young child's activity and play. Settings using such portfolios often invite parents to see them regularly. Some include an evaluation or comments sheet for the parents to comment on what they have seen in the portfolio.

- Involving parents in the Early Years Foundation Stage Profile (EYFSP). It is crucial, once the child is in Reception class, that parents are invited regularly to discuss their child's progress and assessment with the teachers, all of which are integral to the EYFSP process. It acts as a way of keeping parents informed and also takes into account their views, once again involving them in the observation, assessment and planning cycle.

- Giving parents questionnaires that invite them to describe their child's interests and skills enables them indirectly to contribute to the planning of continuous provision.

- An 'open door' policy allows parents to bring their child into the setting, look at displays, be involved in early work and have the opportunity to talk to members of staff.

If parents and teachers can share their knowledge about the child's mathematical development, the implications of this dialogue can be far reaching. Not only can the parent and teacher gain new insight into the child as a developing mathematician, but the teacher will then be able to plan and match continuous provision and focused teaching sessions more appropriately. Similarly, parents may discover different ways in which they can support their child through playful activity at home. Most crucially, however, the family can support the child's view of themselves as an eager and able doer of mathematics.

Involving parents – checklist   ✔

- Do parents feel welcome when they come into the classroom/setting?
- Do all parents feel that their child is included in maths displays and opportunities regardless of their mathematical attainment?
- Is there a range of informative and attractive maths displays to interest parents?
- Are parents able to stand or sit comfortably to read displays, or are the displays situated in a thoroughfare?
- Is there a practitioner available to talk to parents and draw their attention to new maths displays or photos of their child and explain their mathematical significance?
- Are instructions for any early work or the graphics board made clear to all parents?
- Is there an information board to inform parents about maths meetings, family learning courses and other relevant information?
- What opportunities are there for parents to share their observations of their child's mathematical development?
- Are maths story sacks and maths games available in a central place and in a place that will attract parents to them?
- Have all the parents seen recent evidence of their child's engagement in mathematics, either through display or discussion with practitioners?
- Are parents aware of the significance of counting collections, number lines and the graphics area to their child's mathematical development?

Further reading

Arnold, C. (2012) *Improving Your Reflective Practice through Stories of Practitioner Research*. Abingdon: Routledge. Accounts of Pen Green practitioners' research projects are given here, including several about involving families and supporting parents' return to work.

Mairs, K. and Arnold, C. (eds) (2013) *Young Children Learning Through Schemas: Deepening the Dialogue about Learning in the Home and in the Nursery*. Abingdon: Routledge. This text provides accounts of observing and understanding children's schemas and how parents can be involved in supporting them.

Ward, U. (2013) *Working with Parents in Early Years Settings*, 2nd edition. Exeter: Learning Matters. In this book, consideration is given to the relationship between parents and practitioners, with many practical suggestions and case studies. It explores working with other professionals to support all families, particularly those in challenging circumstances.

Whalley, M. and Arnold, C. (2013) *Working with Families in Children's Centres and Early Years Settings*. London: Hodder Education. Written in partnership with the Pen Green Centre, this text provides an overview of current research into work with families, including the use of video in documentation.

Appendices

Photocopiable 1: Independent play

 Role play	• Learning opportunities and curriculum links • Resources	 *Small-world drama*	• Learning opportunities and curriculum links • Resources
 Table-top/pattern making	• Learning opportunities and curriculum links • Resources	 *Reading and listening area*	• Learning opportunities and curriculum links • Resources
 Creative and aesthetic area	• Learning opportunities and curriculum links • Resources	 *Graphics area*	• Learning opportunities and curriculum links • Resources

Mathematics Through Play in the Early Years, Third Edition © Kate Tucker, 2014 (SAGE)

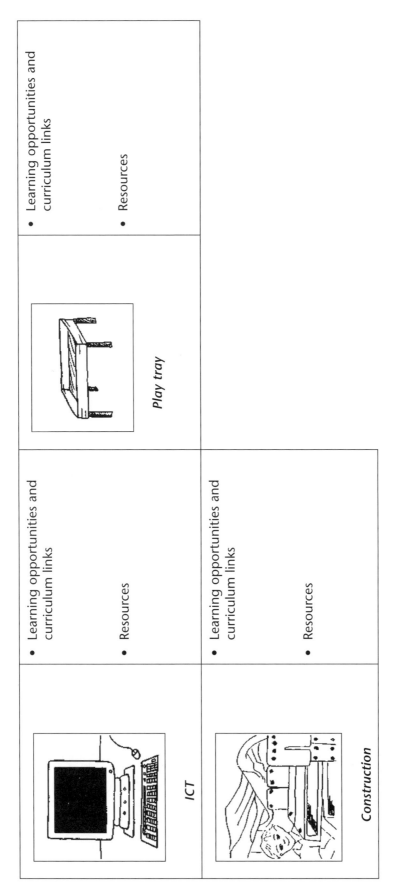

ICT	**Play tray**
• Learning opportunities and curriculum links • Resources	• Learning opportunities and curriculum links • Resources
Construction	
• Learning opportunities and curriculum links • Resources	

Photocopiable 2: Independent play in the outside teaching and learning area

Construction	• Learning opportunities and curriculum links • Resources	PE	• Learning opportunities and curriculum links • Resources
Role play	• Learning opportunities and curriculum links • Resources	Play tray/Sandpit	• Learning opportunities and curriculum links • Resources
Garden/Environment	• Learning opportunities and curriculum links • Resources	Quiet area	• Learning opportunities and curriculum links • Resources

Mathematics Through Play in the Early Years, Third Edition © Kate Tucker, 2014 (SAGE)

Photocopiable 3: Observation sheet for independent play

Date	Name	Learning context	Evidence seen of:							Comments and evidence of: Play and exploring Active play Creating and thinking critically
			CL	PD	PSED	Lit	Maths	UW	EAD	

Mathematics Through Play in the Early Years, Third Edition © Kate Tucker, 2014 (SAGE)

Photocopiable 4: Record and assessment sheet for review time

Date	Name	Activity undertaken (practitioner- or child-initiated?)	Comments on learning (learning dispositions and objectives addressed)

Resources

Chapter 1

Handa's Surprise Browne, Eileen (1994) Walker Books

Chapter 2

Jasper's Beanstalk Butterworth, Nick and Inkpen, Mick (1992) Hodder & Stoughton

Bumpus Jumpus Dinosaurumpus Mitton, Tony and Parker-Rees, Guy (2002) Orchard

Ladybird, Ladybird Brown, Ruth (1998) Andersen Press

The Gruffalo Donaldson, Julia and Scheffler, Axel (1999) Macmillan Children's Books

Jamaica and Brianna Havill, Juanita and O'Brien, Anne Sibley (1994) Heinemann

The Sand Horse Turnbull, Ann and Foreman, Michael (2002) Andersen Press

The Enormous Crocodile Dahl, Roald and Blake, Quentin (1978) Cape

Rosie's Walk Hutchins, Pat (1992) Random Century

The Pet Shop Ahlberg, Allan and Amstutz, Andre (1990) Heinemann

A Bit More Bert Ahlberg, Allan and Briggs, Raymond (2002) Puffin

The Mousehole Cat Barber, Antonia and Bayley, Nicola (1990) Walker Books

Handa's Hen Browne, Eileen (2002) Walker Books

Chapter 3

The Story of Little Babaji Bannerman, Helen and Marcellino, Fred (1997) Ragged Bears

Chapter 4

Numicon®: www.numicon.com

Cameras: www.tts-group.co.uk; www.sony.co.uk; www.digiblue.com

Talking box: www.tts-group.co.uk

Useful storybooks depicting counting, cardinal and ordinal number

My Granny Went to Market: A Round the World Counting Book Blackstone, Stella (1995) Barefoot Books

Mr Magnolia Blake, Quentin (1999) Red Fox

Handa's Hen Browne, Eileen (2002) Walker Books

Engines, Engines Bruce, Lisa (2001) Trafalgar Square

1, 2, 3, to the Zoo: A Counting Book Carle, Eric (1987) Hamish Hamilton

Out for the Count Cave, Kathryn (1991) Frances Lincoln

Ten Green Monsters Clarke, Gus (1993) Andersen Press

One Green Island Hard, Charlotte (1996) Walker Books

Emeka's Gift Oneyefulu, Ifeoma (1995) Frances Lincoln

Addition and subtraction

Five Little Ducks Beck, Ian (1992) Orchard Books

Ten Seeds Brown, Ruth (2001) Andersen Press

Many Hands Counting Book Granstorm, Brita (1999) Walker Books

Ten Red Apples Miller, Virginia (2002) Walker Books

Ten Terrible Pirates Rogers, Paul and Emma (1994) David Bennett

Two Little Witches Ziefert, Harriet (1996) Walker Books

Using money

A Bargain for Frances Hoban, Russell (1992) Mammoth

The Great Pet Sale Inkpen, Mick (1998) Hodder Children's Books

Small Change Lewis, Rob (1992) Red Fox

Bunny Money Wells, Rosemary (1991) Picture Corgi

Multiplication and division

The Doorbell Rang Hutchins, Pat (1986) Bodley Head

One Is a Snail, Ten Is a Crab Sayre, April Pulley et al. (2003) Walker Books

Chapter 5

Bridget Riley: Paintings from the 60s and 70s Corrin, Lisa G., Kudielka, Robert and Spalding, Frances (1999) Serpentine Gallery; www.op-art.co.uk/bridget-riley

African, Indian and Islamic Art: www.geomatrix.co.uk

Andy Goldsworthy Hollis, Jill and Cameron, Ian (1990) Viking; www.goldsworthy.cc.gla.ac.uk

Tom Thumb's Musical Maths MacGregor, Helen (1998) A & C Black

www.artcyclopedia.com/artists/klee_paul.html

www.digiblue.com (digital microscope)

www.morrissociety.org

www.rm.com; www.interactive-education.co.uk (visualizers)

www.smartteach.com (SMART interactive table)

Useful storybooks depicting pattern

What Goes Snap? Boyle, Alison and Gale, Cathy (1998) Walker Books

The Very Hungry Caterpillar Carle, Eric (1970) Hamilton

Kings of Another Country French, Fiona (1992) Oxford University Press

Nikos the Fisherman French, Fiona (1995) Oxford University Press

Mrs Mopple's Washing Line Hewett, Anita (1994) Red Fox

Ten Bright Eyes Hindley, Judy (1998) Leveinson

Lucy and Tom's 1, 2, 3 Hughes, Shirley (1989) Puffin

Curious Clownfish Maddern, Eric (1990) Frances Lincoln

Elmer McKee, David (1990) Red Fox

My Mum and Dad Make Me Laugh Sharratt, Nick (1994) Walker Books

Chapter 6

The Big Concrete Lorry Hughes, Shirley (1989) Walker

Snail Trail Brown, Ruth (2000) Andersen

Traffic Jam Owen, Annie (1990) Orchard Books

Come Away From the Water, Shirley Burningham, John (1977) Cape

Jack's Fantastic Voyage Foreman, Michael (1994) Red Fox

Katie Morag and the Two Grandmothers Hedderwick, Mairi (1985) Bodley Head

Mondrian Deicher, Susanne (2001) Midpoint Press

Barbara Hepworth Gale, Matthew and Stephens, Chris (2001) Tate Gallery Publishing

Spy Shapes in Art Micklethwait, Lucy (2004) Collins

www.apple.com (Apple TV)

www.communityplaythings.com (Community Playthings)

Useful storybooks showing shape and space

Brown Rabbit's Shape Book Baker, Alan (1994) Kingfisher

If At First You Do Not See Brown, Ruth (1982) Sparrow

The Secret Birthday Message Carle, Eric (1972) Hamish Hamilton

Little Cloud Carle, Eric (1998) Puffin

The Shape of Things Dodds Dale, Ann (1994) Walker

The Wheeling and Whirling-Around Book Hindley, Judy and Chamberlain, Margaret (1994) Walker

Changes, Changes Hutchins, Pat (1994) Red Fox

Grandfather Tang's Story Tompert, Ann (1991) MacRae

The Shape Game Browne, Anthony (2003) Doubleday

Chapter 7

Dartfish: www.dartfish.com

Datalogger: www.impress-sensors.co.uk

Lasy®: www.lasy.com

Useful storybooks about weight and capacity

Who Sank the Boat? Mien, Pamela (1982) Hamilton

The Lighthouse Keeper's Catastrophe Armitage, Ronda and David (1986) Deutsch

Mr Gumpy's Outing Burningham, John (2001) Red Fox

Honey Biscuits Hooper, Meredith (1997) Kingfisher

Length, distance and height

Rosie's Walk Hutchins, Pat (1992) Random Century

Six Feet Long and Three Feet Wide Billington, Jeannie and Smee, Nicola (1999) Walker Books

Jim and the Beanstalk Briggs, Raymond (1970) Hamilton

Hue Boy Mitchell, Rita Phillips (1992) Gollancz

Time

The Bad-Tempered Ladybird Carle, Eric (1997) Hamilton

Tick-Tock Dunbar, James (1996) Franklin Watts

Mr Wolf's Week Hawkins, Colin (1997) Picture Lions

The Stopwatch Lloyd, David (1986) Walker Books

The School Bus Comes at Eight O'Clock McKee, David (1993) Andersen Press

Chapter 8

Bear's Adventure Blathwayt, Benedict (1988) MacRae

The Lighthouse Keeper's Lunch Armitage, Rhonda and David (2007) Scholastic

Useful websites for research, curriculum, planning and assessment

Association of Mathematics Teachers: www.atm.org.uk

British Society for Research into Learning Mathematics: www.bsrlm.org.uk

Children's Mathematics: www.childrens-mathematics.net

Curriculum for Excellence, Scotland: www.acurriculumforexcellencescotland.gov.uk

Department for Education: www.education.gov.uk

Foundation Phase, Wales: www.wales.gov.uk/foundationphase

Foundation Years: www.foundationyears.org.uk

National Centre for Excellence in the Teaching of Mathematics: www.ncetm.org.uk

The Mathematical Association: www.m-a.org.uk

Times Educational Supplement: www.tes.co.uk

References

Alexander, R. (2009) *Towards a New Primary Curriculum: A Report from the Cambridge Primary Review. Part 2: The Future.* Cambridge: University of Cambridge.

Athey, C. (1990) *Extending Thought in Your Children: A Parent–Teacher Partnership.* London: Paul Chapman Publishing.

Bilton, H. (2010) *Outdoor Learning in the Early Years: Management and Innovation,* 3rd edition. Abingdon: Routledge.

Bronson, M. (2000) *Self-regulation in Early Childhood: Nature and Nurture.* New York: Guilford Press.

Bruce, T. (1991) *Time to Play in Early Childhood Education.* London: Hodder & Stoughton.

Bruner, J. (1991) 'The nature and uses of immaturity', in M. Woodhead, R. Carr and R. Light (eds) *Becoming a Person.* London: Routledge/Open University Press, pp. 247–72.

Carruthers, E. and Worthington, M. (2011) *Understanding Children's Mathematical Graphics: Beginnings in Play.* Maidenhead: Open University Press/McGraw-Hill.

Cubey, P. (1999) 'Exploring block play: a study of block play in three early childhood centres in England in January 1998', *Early Childhood Practice,* 1(1): 6–27.

Department of Children, Schools and Families (DCSF) (2008) *Independent Review of Mathematics Teaching in Early Years Settings and Primary Schools.* Available at: http://webarchive.nationalarchives. gov.uk/20130401151715/https://www.education.gov.uk/publications/eOrderingDownload/ Williams%20Mathematics.pdf (accessed June 2013).

Desforges, C. (2003) *The Impact of Parental Involvement, Parental Support and Family Education on Pupil Achievement and Adjustment* (Research Report 433). London: Department for Education and Schools.

Department for Education (DfE) (2011) *Supporting Families in the Foundation Years.* London: Department for Education and Department of Health.

Department for Education (DfE) (2012) *Statutory Framework for the Early Years Foundation Stage: Setting the Standards for Learning, Development and Care for Children from Birth to Five.* London: Department for Education.

Department for Education and Employment (DfEE) (1999) *The National Numeracy Strategy.* London: Department for Education and Employment.

Department for Education and Skills (DfES) (2006) *Primary Framework for Literacy and Mathematics.* Norwich: Department for Education and Skills.

Field, F. (2010) *The Foundation Years: Preventing Poor Children Becoming Poor Adults – The Report of the Independent Review on Poverty and Life Chances.* London: Cabinet Office.

Fisher, J. (2010) *Moving on to Key Stage 1: Improving Transition from the Early Years Foundation Stage.* Maidenhead: Open University Press.

Gersten, N., Jordan, C. and Flojo, J.R. (2005) 'Early identification and interventions for students with mathematics difficulties', *Journal of Learning Disabilities,* 38(4): 293–304.

Gifford, S. (2008) '"How do you teach nursery children mathematics?" In search of a mathematics pedagogy for the early years', in I. Thompson (ed.) *Teaching and Learning Early Number*, 2nd edition. Maidenhead: Open University Press, pp. 217–26.

Gura, R. (ed.) (1992) *Exploring Learning: Young Children and Blockplay*. London: Paul Chapman Publishing.

Haylock, D. and Cockburn, A. (2013) *Understanding Mathematics for Young Children*, 4th edition. London: Sage Publications.

Knight, S. (2011) *Risk and Adventure in Early Years Outdoor Play: Learning from Forest Schools*. London: Sage Publications.

Montague-Smith, A. and Price, A.J. (2012) *Mathematics in Early Years Education*. London: Routledge.

National Advisory Committee on Creativity and Cultural Education (NACCCE) (1999) *All Our Futures: Creativity, Culture and Education*. London: Department for Education and Employment/Department for Culture, Media and Sport.

Office for Standards in Education (Ofsted) (2004) *Transition for the Reception Year to Year 1: An Evaluation by HMI*. London: Ofsted.

Piaget, J. (1958) *The Child's Construction of Reality*. London: Routledge & Kegan Paul.

Pound, L. (2008) *Thinking and Learning about Mathematics in the Early Years*. London: Routledge.

Pratt, N. (2011) 'Mathematics outside the classroom', in S. Waite (ed.) *Children Learning Outside the Classroom: From Birth to Eleven*. London: Sage Publications, pp. 80–93.

Rose, J. (2009) Independent Review of the Primary Curriculum: Final Report. Available at: http://www.educationengland.org.uk/documents/pdfs/2009-IRPC-final-report.pdf (accessed June 2013).

Scottish Executive (SE) (2007) A Curriculum for Excellence: Building the Curriculum 2 – Active Learning in the Early Years. Available at: http://www.educationscotland.gov.uk/images/Building_the_Curriculum_2_tcm4-408069.pdf (accessed June 2013).

Siraj-Blatchford, I., Silva, K., Mutlock, S., Gilden, R. and Bell, D. (2002) *Researching Effective Pedagogy in the Early Years* (Research Report 356). London: Department for Education and Skills.

Smilansky, S. and Shefatya, L. (1990) *Facilitating Play: A Medium for Promoting Cognitive, Socioemotional and Academic Development in Young Children*. Gaithersburg, MD: Psychological and Educational Publications.

Stewart, N. (2011) *How Children Learn: The Characteristics of Effective Early Learning*. London: The British Association for Early Childhood Education.

Tickell, C. (2011) *The Early Years: Foundations for Life, Health and Learning – An Independent Report on the Early Years Foundation Stage to Her Majesty's Government*. London: Department for Education.

Vygotsky, L.S. (1978) *Mind in Society*, translated and edited by M. Cole, V. John-Steiner, S. Scribner and E. Souberman. Cambridge, MA: Harvard University Press.

Welsh Assembly Government (WAG) (2008) *Framework for Children's Learning for 3 to 7 Year Olds in Wales*. Cardiff: WAG.

Whalley, M. (2007) *Involving Parents in their Children's Learning*, 2nd edition. London: Paul Chapman Publishing.

Index

Added to a page number 'f' denotes a figure, 't' denotes a table and 'g' denotes glossary. Entries in bold refer to activities.